Neuropharmacology

Neuropharmacology

Revathi Boyina
M.Pharm, Ph.D
Associate Professor and HOD
Department of Pharmacology
QIS College of Pharmacy, Ongole.

Sreya Kosanam
Pharm D
Faculty of Pharmacy,
Department of Pharmacy Practice
Dr. M. G. R Educational and Research Institute, Chennai.

Marri Jalaiah
M.Pharm, Ph.D.,
Associate Professor and HOD
Department of Pharmacy Practice
QIS College of Pharmacy, Ongole.

D. Dhachinamoorthi
M.Pharm, Ph.D.,
Professor & Principal,
Sree Abirami College of Pharmacy, Coimbatore.

Pharma Med PRESS
An Imprint of
BSP Books Pvt. Ltd

™ **PharmaMed Press**
An imprint of BSP Books Pvt. Ltd
4-4-309/316, Giriraj Lane,
Sultan Bazar, Hyderabad - 500 095.

Neuropharmacology
by **Revathi Boyina, Sreya Kosanam, Marri Jalaiah and D. Dhachinamoorthi**

Published by:

™ **PharmaMed Press**

An imprint of BSP Books Pvt. Ltd.
4-4-309/316, Giriraj Lane, Sultan Bazar, Hyderabad - 500 095.
Phone: 040-23445688; Fax: 91+40-23445611
E-mail: info@pharmamedpress.net
www.bspbooks.net/www.pharmamedpress.net

ISBN: 978-93-48734-44-0 (Paperback)

PREFACE

A book on Neuropharmacology explains how medications affect the neurological system. This book covers the information about neurohumoral transmission in autonomic nervous system. Next chapter focus on drugs acting on autonomic nervous system and subdivisions of autonomic nervous system. The mechanism of action, (pharmacodynamics) as well as absorption, distribution, metabolism and excretion (pharmacokinetics) along with the adverse effects, clinical uses, interactions, doses, contraindications and routes of administration of the drugs were elaborated. Next part of focus on the neurohumoral transmission in central nervous system and different drug targets in central nervous system. Next chapter focus on the psychopharmacology of drugs acting on central nervous system. Another section focuses on drugs used in pain management, neurological disorders, cognitive and memory enhancers. Next chapter focus on the future challenges of neuropharmacology and advances in neurological disorders treatment using gene therapy. This book is designed for students, researchers, and clinicians interested in neuropharmacology, whether they are just beginning to explore the field or seeking a deeper understanding of its current state and future directions.

This is the first book with exclusive focus on Neuropharmacology. Complete and a concise information of nervous system drugs is available. The book is covering the syllabus of drugs acting on nervous system in Pharmacy, Medical and Nursing course. Special focus psychopharmacology of drugs, neurological disorders (Parkinson's and Alzheimer's disease where the researchers are focusing. The book also provides the advances in neurological disorders treatment.

The author's tried the best to make the content concise and covering all the topics for ease of understanding and interesting to students.

Above all, we would want to thank all of the supporters and publishers, PharmMed Press for bringing out such a high-quality book.

- Authors

Contents

Chapter 6

Antidepressants

Chapter 7

Drugs used in Pain Management

Chapter 8

Neurological Disorders

Chapter 9

Cognitive and Memory Enhancement

Chapter 10

Future Directions and Challenges of Neuropharmacology

CHAPTER 1

Introduction of Neuropharmacology

The study of known endogenous and exogenous chemical agents' effects on the neurobiological processes in the mammalian nervous system is known as neuropharmacology. The most significant physiological feature that distinguishes humans from other animals is brain function. Pharmacological intervention is a crucial component in treating brain function disorders, which are a serious concern for human society. These disorders can arise from primary or secondary malfunctions of other systems. Neuroactive substances can be hormones, enzymes, or neurotransmitters in their natural condition. In a clinical context, a neuroactive agent is a drug a term with widespread usage but often ambiguous definitions. The endocrine system uses changes in blood-borne hormone levels to communicate with specific tissues. On the other hand, the nervous system influences behaviour by quickly sending electrical impulses along nerve fibres that end at effector cells, which react only when neuromodulator substances are released. Medications that mimic or change the functions in order to achieve their main therapeutic impact. The basic physiology of the nervous system is explained, along with the function of neurotransmitters in the transmission of messages between intracellular chemical changes and extracellular events. There are two distinct parts to the nervous system: the peripheral nervous system, which consists of neurons outside the brain and spinal cord, or any nerves that enter or leave the central nervous system (CNS), and the central nervous system (CNS), which is made up of the brain and spinal cord.

The peripheral nervous system is divided into two parts: the efferent division, which transports signals from the brain and spinal cord to peripheral tissues, and the afferent division, which transports information from the periphery to the CNS. Afferent neurons give sensory input to influence the function of the efferent division via reflex arcs, which are neuronal circuits that mediate a reflex action. The efferent component of the peripheral nervous system is further divided into two major functional subdivisions: somatic and autonomic systems. Somatic efferent neurons have a role in the voluntary control of processes like skeletal muscle contraction, which is required for locomotion. Conversely, the autonomic system controls everyday needs for essential body processes without conscious mental intervention. It is made up of efferent neurons that innervate the exocrine glands, as well as the vascular and smooth muscles of the viscera cardiac muscle. This allows it to regulate blood flow, digestion, cardiac output, and glandular secretions.

The difficulty of comprehending how medications affect the central nervous system (CNS) is particularly difficult for two reasons. The first is that medications with core actions are particularly important to humanity. They are the drugs that people most frequently give themselves for non-medical purposes (e.g., alcohol, tea and coffee, cannabis, nicotine, opiates, amphetamines, and so on). They are also of great therapeutic importance. The second reason is that comprehending the effects of drugs is significantly more challenging since the central nervous system (CNS) is functionally far more complicated than any other system in the body.

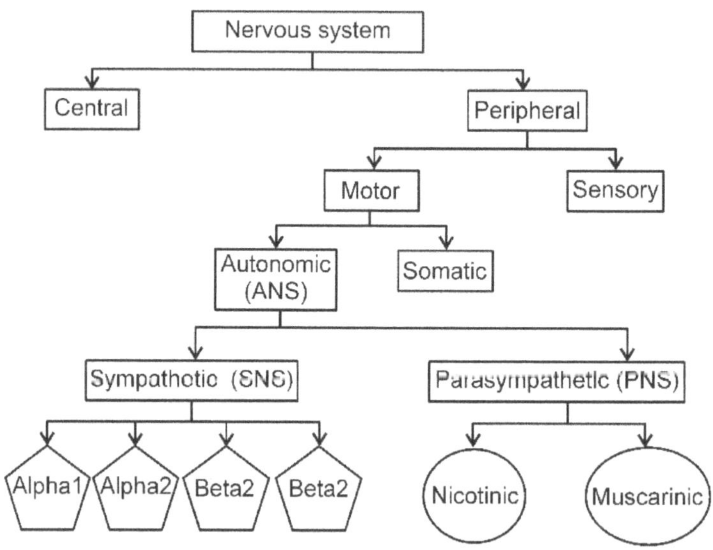

CHAPTER 2

Neurohumoral Transmission in Autonomic Nervous System

In the autonomic nervous system (ANS), neurohumoral transmission refers to the communication between neurons and their target cells, which can be smooth muscle, cardiac muscle, or gland cells. The ANS is responsible for regulating involuntary bodily functions such as heart rate, digestion, respiratory rate, and pupillary response.

Neurohumoral transmission in the ANS involves the release of neurotransmitters from preganglionic neurons onto postganglionic neurons in ganglia (ganglionic transmission) and the release of neurotransmitters or hormones from postganglionic neurons onto target cells (neuroeffector transmission).

The ANS consists of two main divisions: the sympathetic nervous system (SNS) and the parasympathetic nervous system (PNS), each of which has distinct neurotransmitters involved in neurohumoral transmission:

1. **Sympathetic Nervous System (SNS):**
   - Preganglionic neurons release acetylcholine (ACh) onto nicotinic acetylcholine receptors (nAChRs) in sympathetic ganglia.
   - Postganglionic neurons release norepinephrine (noradrenaline) onto adrenergic receptors in target tissues.
   - Adrenal medulla releases epinephrine (adrenaline) and norepinephrine into the bloodstream as hormones, which then act on target tissues throughout the body.
2. **Parasympathetic Nervous System (PNS):**
   - Preganglionic neurons release acetylcholine (ACh) onto nicotinic acetylcholine receptors (nAChRs) in parasympathetic ganglia.
   - Postganglionic neurons release acetylcholine (ACh) onto muscarinic acetylcholine receptors (mAChRs) in target tissues.

The balance between sympathetic and parasympathetic activity regulates the homeostasis of various physiological processes. Dysregulation of neurohumoral transmission in the autonomic nervous system can lead to various disorders, including hypertension, heart rhythm abnormalities, gastrointestinal disorders, and autonomic neuropathies.

2.1 MAJOR MEDIATORS, NEUROTRANSMITTERS AND THEIR FUNCTIONS IN ANS

In the autonomic nervous system (ANS), several neurotransmitters and mediators play key roles in transmitting signals between neurons and their target cells. Here are the major mediators, neurotransmitters, and their functions in the ANS:

1. **Acetylcholine (ACh):**
   - **Functions:**
     - Acts as the primary neurotransmitter released by preganglionic neurons in both the sympathetic and parasympathetic divisions of the ANS.
     - Stimulates nicotinic acetylcholine receptors (nAChRs) on postganglionic neurons in autonomic ganglia.
     - Stimulates muscarinic acetylcholine receptors (mAChRs) on target cells in parasympathetic target tissues.
2. **Norepinephrine (Noradrenaline):**
   - **Functions**:
     - Acts as the primary neurotransmitter released by most postganglionic sympathetic neurons.
     - Stimulates adrenergic receptors (alpha and beta receptors) on target tissues, such as smooth muscle in blood vessels, heart, and glands.
     - Mediates sympathetic responses including increased heart rate, pupil dilation, and vasoconstriction.
3. **Epinephrine (Adrenaline):**
   - **Functions**:
     - Released from the adrenal medulla into the bloodstream as a hormone in response to sympathetic activation.

- Acts on adrenergic receptors throughout the body, producing effects similar to norepinephrine but with a broader systemic impact.
- Enhances the "fight or flight" response, increasing heart rate, blood pressure, and metabolic rate.

4. **Dopamine:**
   - **Functions**:
     - Acts as a neurotransmitter in certain parts of the ANS, particularly in the sympathetic nervous system.
     - Dopaminergic neurons project from the hypothalamus to regulate functions such as blood pressure, renal function, and hormone release.

5. **Other Functions Neuromodulators:**
   - **Functions**:
   - Various other neurotransmitters and neuropeptides play modulatory roles in the ANS, including serotonin, histamine, substance P, neuropeptide Y, and nitric oxide (NO).
   - These substances can modulate the activity of autonomic neurons, influencing functions such as gastrointestinal motility, pain perception, and cardiovascular regulation.

The balance and interaction between these neurotransmitters and mediators regulate autonomic functions and maintain homeostasis in the body. Dysregulation of these signaling pathways can contribute to various autonomic disorders, including hypertension, dysautonomia, and gastrointestinal motility disorders.

2.2 TYPES AND FUNCTIONS OF NEURORECEPTORS IN ANS

This peripheral nervous system, which controls involuntary body activities, includes the autonomic nervous system (ANS). The nerve systems of the parasympathetic and sympathetic branches comprise its two primary divisions. Mediating the actions of neurotransmitters in the ANS is a critical function of neuroreceptors. A summary of the many kinds and purposes of the neuroreceptors involved are provided below:

Types of Neuroreceptors in the ANS

1. **Cholinergic Receptors**
   - **Nicotinic Receptors**

Purposes of the neuroreceptors involved are provided below:

- **Location:** Found at the neuromuscular junction, autonomic ganglia, and the adrenal medulla.
- **Function:** Mediate fast synaptic transmission. When acetylcholine binds, it opens ion channels that allow sodium ions to flow into the cell, leading to depolarization and muscle contraction or neuronal activation.

o **Muscarinic Receptors**

- **Location:** Located in various target tissues, including the heart, smooth muscle, and glands.
- **Function:** Mediate slower, longer-lasting responses. They activate G-protein coupled pathways, leading to various effects such as decreased heart rate (M2 receptor) or increased glandular secretion (M3 receptor).

2. **Adrenergic Receptors**

o **Alpha (α) Receptors**

- **Location:** Found in blood vessels, smooth muscles, and various organs.
- **Function:** Generally promote vasoconstriction (α1 receptors) and inhibit neurotransmitter release (α2 receptors), leading to increased blood pressure and reduced sympathetic outflow.

o **Beta (β) Receptors**

- **Location:** Present in the heart, lungs, and other tissues.
- **Function:**
- **β1:** Increases heart rate and contractility.
- **β2:** Promotes bronchodilation and vasodilation in skeletal muscle.
- **β3:** Involved in lipolysis and thermogenesis in adipose tissue.

Functions of Neuroreceptors in the ANS

- **Regulation of Heart Rate and Cardiac Output:**

o Cholinergic and adrenergic receptors in the heart modulate heart rate and contractility, balancing sympathetic stimulation (increased heart rate via β1) and parasympathetic inhibition (decreased heart rate via M2).

- **Control of Smooth Muscle Activity:**

o Neuroreceptors in smooth muscle tissues regulate contraction and relaxation. For example, α1 receptors cause vasoconstriction, while β2 receptors promote relaxation of bronchial and vascular smooth muscle.

- **Glandular Secretion:**
  - Muscarinic receptors control secretion from glands (like salivary and sweat glands) in response to parasympathetic stimulation.
- **Metabolic Regulation:**
  - Adrenergic receptors influence metabolism, such as increasing blood glucose levels and mobilizing energy stores through β3 receptors.
- **Stress Response:**
  - During stress, the sympathetic nervous system activates adrenergic receptors, resulting in increased heart rate, blood flow to muscles, and energy availability (fight or flight response).

Neuroreceptors in the ANS are essential for maintaining homeostasis and enabling appropriate physiological responses to environmental changes. Understanding these receptors helps in pharmacological approaches to treat various autonomic dysfunctions and related conditions.

CHAPTER 3

Neuropharmacology of Drugs Acting on Autonomic Nervous System (ANS)

3.1 ADRENERGIC AND ANTIADRENERGIC DRUGS ADRENERGIC DRUGS

Adrenergic drugs, also known as sympathomimetics, stimulate the sympathetic nervous system by mimicking the action of endogenous catecholamines like norepinephrine, epinephrine, and dopamine. These drugs act on adrenergic receptors and are classified into

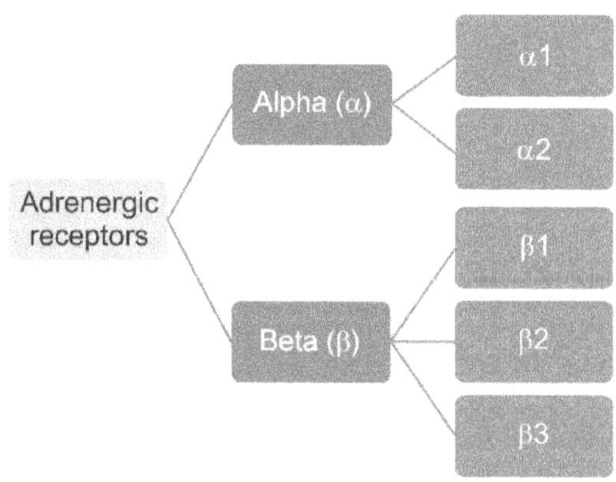

ADRENERGIC DRUGS (Sympathomimetics)

These drugs mimic the actions of endogenous catecholamines. They are classified into three sub-groups as follows:

1. Directly acting sympathomimetics
2. Indirectly acting sympathomimetics
3. Mixed action sympathomimetics

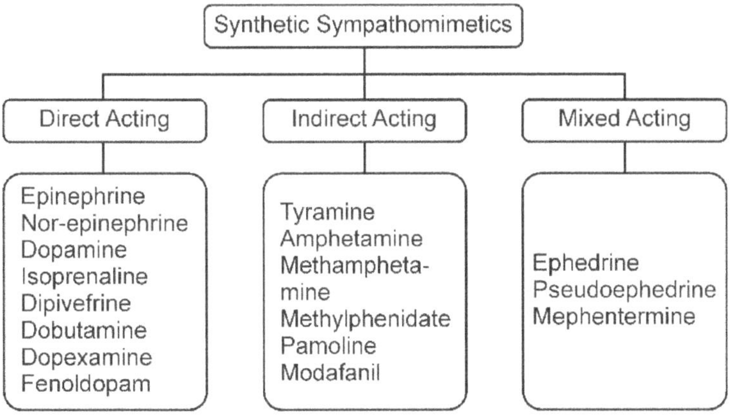

1. Directly Acting Sympathomimetics:

Directly Acting Sympathomimetics are two types:

Catecholamines

a. Endogenous
b. Synthetic

Non-Catecholamines

Overview

Epinephrine is a catecholamine produced in the adrenal medulla from tyrosine. It acts on both alpha (α) and beta (β) receptors, influencing various physiological responses.

Actions

1. Cardiovascular Effects

- **Heart:** Increases heart rate and contractility via β1 receptors, raising cardiac output and oxygen demand.
- **Vascular System:** At low doses, it causes vasodilation (β2 effect) in muscles and the liver; at high doses, it induces vasoconstriction (α effect) in skin and organs, leading to higher systolic blood pressure and slightly lower diastolic pressure.

2. Respiratory Effects

- **Bronchodilation:** Relaxes bronchial muscles through β2 receptors, reversing bronchoconstriction and aiding in conditions like anaphylaxis and asthma attacks.
- **Histamine Release:** Inhibits the release of histamines from mast cells.

3. Metabolic Effects

- **Hyperglycemia:** Increases blood sugar levels by promoting glycogen breakdown (β2 effect), stimulating glucagon release (β2 effect), and decreasing insulin release (α2 effect).
- **Lipolysis:** Activates lipolysis in adipose tissue via β receptors, increasing free fatty acids and glycerol through the cAMP pathway.

Therapeutic Uses

- **Bronchospasm:** Epinephrine is the main medication used in emergencies for respiratory issues caused by bronchoconstriction, such as acute asthma and anaphylactic shock.
- **Anaphylactic shock:** Epinephrine is the preferred treatment for Type I hypersensitivity reactions caused by allergens.
- **Cardiac arrest:** Epinephrine may be used to restore cardiac rhythm in patients with cardiac arrest regardless of the cause.

Pharmacokinetics: Epinephrine acts quickly but has a short duration of effect because it is rapidly broken down. The best route for administration is intramuscularly in the anterior thigh, as this allows for quick absorption. In emergencies, it can be given intravenously (IV) for the fastest response.

Adverse Effects

- **CNS Disturbances:** Epinephrine may cause negative effects on the central nervous system, including anxiety, fear, tension, headaches, and tremors.
- **Hemorrhage:** The drug can lead to cerebral hemorrhage due to a significant increase in blood pressure.
- **Cardiac Arrhythmias:** Epinephrine can trigger irregular heartbeats, especially in patients taking digoxin.
- **Pulmonary Edema:** Epinephrine can induce pulmonary edema.

Interactions

- **Hyperthyroidism:** In patients with hyperthyroidism, epinephrine may have stronger cardiovascular effects.
- **Cocaine:** When cocaine is present, epinephrine can cause intensified cardiovascular effects because cocaine inhibits the reuptake of catecholamines into adrenergic neurons.
- **Diabetes:** Epinephrine stimulates the release of glucose from the body's stores. For diabetic patients, this may necessitate an increase in insulin dosage.

- **β-Blockers:** These medications block epinephrine's effects on β receptors, which can lead to unopposed stimulation of other receptors. This may result in increased peripheral resistance and elevated blood pressure.

i. **Norepinephrine (Nor-Adrenaline) (Ne/Na):** Endogenous norepinephrine (NE) exists primarily as the l-isomer, which is more potent than the d-isomer. NE mainly targets alpha (α) receptors, with the following receptor affinity: $\alpha 1 = \alpha 2 > \beta 1 >> \beta 2$. It also has significant effects on β3 receptors.

Cardiovascular Actions: Norepinephrine increases both systolic and diastolic blood pressure through cardiac stimulation (via β1 receptors) and by raising peripheral vascular resistance (via α1 receptors). Norepinephrine primarily exhibits α effects and does not demonstrate Dale's vasomotor reversal.

Therapeutic Uses

Norepinephrine is cautiously used to treat cardiogenic shock, as this condition leads to increased vascular resistance and reduced blood flow to essential organs.

Adverse Effects, Precautions, and Contraindications: The adverse effects of norepinephrine (NE) are like those of epinephrine (adrenaline).

ii. **DOPAMINE:** Dopamine is an endogenous catecholamine that does not cross the blood-brain barrier when given parenterally, thus lacking central nervous system effects. At therapeutic intravenous doses of 2-5 µg/kg/min, it primarily activates D1 receptors, leading to renal vasodilation, increased glomerular filtration rate (GFR), and enhanced renal blood flow. At 5-10 µg/kg/min, it stimulates β1 receptors, increasing cardiac contractility and heart rate without changing total peripheral resistance or mean blood pressure due to concurrent renal and splanchnic vasodilation. Doses above 10 µg/kg/min can activate α receptors, resulting in vasoconstriction and negating the benefits of lower doses.

Therapeutic Uses

It is used in conditions of low cardiac output with compromised renal functions, such as cardiogenic shock due to myocardial infarction, trauma, or surgery. It is also used in the treatment of congestive heart failure renal and liver failure.

Adverse Effects

They include nausea, vomiting, tachycardia, ectopic beats, hypertension (only in high doses), and cardiac arrhythmia (low incidence).

Synthetic Catecholamines

These are synthetic catecholamines containing two adjacent hydroxyl groups in the benzene nucleus.

A) **ISOPRENALINE:** It predominantly stimulates ß1- and ß2-adrenoceptors. It has negligible a-receptor action.

Pharmacological / Cardiovascular Effects

Isoprenaline exerts positive inotropic and chronotropic effects on the heart, leading to increased cardiac output via β1 receptor activation. This cardiac stimulation may cause a slight increase in systolic blood pressure while mean arterial pressure and diastolic blood pressure are significantly reduced. Isoprenaline also relaxes arterioles in skeletal muscle through β2 receptor effects, decreasing peripheral resistance. Additionally, it relaxes bronchial and gastrointestinal smooth muscles, alleviating broncho-constriction mainly by stimulating β2 receptors and partially by inhibiting histamine release.

Pharmacokinetics

Isoprenaline is well absorbed when administered parenterally or as an aerosol.

Therapeutic Uses

Isoprenaline is used primarily in emergency situations to increase heart rate in patients experiencing bradycardia or heart block, particularly before the insertion of an artificial pacemaker.

Adverse Effects

The cardiac stimulant effects of isoprenaline can result in palpitations, sinus tachycardia, or even serious arrhythmias.

B) **DOBUTAMINE:** Dobutamine is a racemic mixture of two enantiomers: the l-form is a strong α1 receptor agonist, while the d-form is a potent α1 antagonist and a powerful β1 receptor agonist. This results in mixed cardiovascular effects, primarily enhancing inotropic (contractility) rather than chronotropic (heart rate) effects without significantly altering peripheral vascular resistance or blood pressure. Dobutamine increases cardiac output and stroke volume while maintaining heart rate and blood pressure. Due to its short half-life of about 2 minutes, it is usually administered via intravenous infusion.

Therapeutic Uses

Dobutamine is administered to treat patients with heart failure related to myocardial infarction, during cardiac surgery, and for short-term management of acute congestive heart failure.

Adverse Effects

Dobutamine can cause a sharp rise in blood pressure and heart rate in patients with hypertension. As an inotropic agent, it increases myocardial oxygen demand, which may precipitate angina or worsen myocardial infarction. Tolerance may develop with prolonged use. Due to its effect on increasing atrioventricular (AV) conduction, it should be used cautiously in patients with atrial fibrillation.

Adverse Effects

Common side effects include:

- Reflex tachycardia
- Increased intraocular pressure
- Headaches

Additionally, hypokalemia may occur due to its diuretic effects.

NON-CATECHOLAMINES or INDIRECTLY ACTING SYPATHOMIMETICS

Non-catecholamines are drugs that contain only one hydroxyl group and a substituted amine on the benzene nucleus. While they are not classified as catecholamines, they still exhibit agonistic activity at alpha (α) receptors. These drugs can be divided into two categories: **α1-agonists** and **α2-agonists**.

Common drugs in this category include:

A) **TYRAMINE:** Tyramine is not used for clinical purposes but is commonly found in foods such as cheese, beef, wine, beer, bananas, yeast, and yogurt. It is metabolized by monoamine oxidase (MAO) present in the liver, gastrointestinal tract, and other body tissues. If a patient is taking any MAO inhibitor, consuming tyramine-containing substances can lead to a serious hypertensive crisis due to the excessive release of norepinephrine (NE) from storage sites.

B) **AMPHETAMINE:** Amphetamine acts as a powerful central nervous system (CNS) stimulant and also exerts effects on both peripheral alpha (α) and beta (β) adrenergic receptors.

Mechanism of Action

Amphetamine enters nerve endings via active transport, displacing dopamine (DA) and norepinephrine (NE) from their storage vesicles by altering vesicular pH. It inhibits monoamine oxidase B (MAO-B), raising intra-neuronal dopamine levels and promoting its release through reverse transport. This ultimately increases dopamine concentration in the synaptic cleft.

Pharmacokinetics

Amphetamine is well absorbed orally and crosses the blood-brain barrier, with a considerable portion excreted unmetabolized in urine. Its clearance can be enhanced by acidifying the urine with substances like ascorbic acid or ammonium chloride, which reduces the drug's reabsorption.

CNS Effects

The D-isomer of amphetamine, dextroamphetamine, is 3-4 times more potent than the L-isomer for central nervous system (CNS) stimulation. It enhances wakefulness and alertness while reducing CNS depression but does not eliminate the need for sleep. Repeated use can lead to amphetamine psychosis, resembling schizophrenia, characterized by paranoid thoughts and hallucinations, while higher doses may increase aggressiveness and the risk of violent behavior.

CVS Effects: The L-isomer of amphetamine is more potent than the D-isomer regarding cardiovascular effects, increasing both systolic and diastolic blood pressure while causing tachycardia, which may be followed by bradycardia. Higher doses can lead to arrhythmias.

Effects on Smooth Muscle: Amphetamine constricts the urinary bladder sphincter, causing difficulty in urination while also relaxing the gut and increasing uterine tone.

Other Effects: It suppresses appetite by depressing the lateral hypothalamic feeding center, but tolerance to this effect develops quickly, making it unsuitable for appetite suppression.

Therapeutic Uses

Amphetamine is indicated for the following conditions:

- **Narcolepsy:** In small doses, amphetamine helps improve narcolepsy and prevents daytime sleep attacks. It is recommended that the drug not be administered after 4:00 PM to avoid disrupting nighttime sleep, which can lead to excessive daytime sleepiness.

- **Attention Deficit Hyperactivity Disorder (ADHD):** This condition is often observed in children and is characterized by impulsiveness, difficulty in interpersonal relationships, excitability, and challenges in sustaining attention, which can result in academic setbacks. Interestingly, some children with ADHD respond positively to low doses of amphetamine.

Adverse Effects

Amphetamine can cause a variety of adverse effects, including:

- **Central Nervous System (CNS) Effects:** Restlessness, tremors, hyperactive reflexes, irritability, insomnia, euphoria, hallucinations, and sweating. High doses can lead to psychosis.
- **Cardiovascular Effects:** Palpitations, headaches, and arrhythmias.
- **Gastrointestinal Effects:** Dry mouth, a metallic taste, loss of appetite (anorexia), abdominal cramps, and difficulty urinating.
- **Dependence and Tolerance:** Prolonged use can lead to psychological dependence. Tolerance develops to the appetite-suppressing effects, but not for narcolepsy. Withdrawal symptoms may include CNS depression, insomnia, and tremors.

Treatment of Toxicity

Amphetamine toxicity can be managed by acidifying the urine using ammonium chloride or ascorbic acid. This approach prevents the reabsorption of amphetamine in the renal tubules and promotes its excretion. Diazepam may also be administered to mitigate adverse effects on the central nervous system (CNS).

MIXED ACTION SYMPATHOMIMETICS

Mixed action sympathomimetics function similarly to indirectly acting sympathomimetics by replacing stores of norepinephrine (NE). In addition to this effect, they also have a direct action on both alpha (α) and beta (β) receptors, similar to norepinephrine (NE) and epinephrine (E).

The following drugs are classified under this category:

- **Ephedrine**
- **Pseudoephedrine**
- **Phenylpropanolamine**

- **Amphetamine** (to some extent, as it also has mixed actions)

These drugs are often used for various therapeutic purposes, including respiratory conditions, nasal congestion, and stimulants.

(a) EPHEDRINE: Ephedrine, derived from *Ephedra vulgaris*, is a non-catecholamine alkaloid that acts on both alpha (α) and beta (β) receptors while enhancing norepinephrine (NE) release. Unlike epinephrine and norepinephrine, it is not broken down by monoamine oxidase (MAO) or catechol-O-methyltransferase (COMT), resulting in a longer action duration. Ephedrine stimulates heart rate, cardiac output, and blood pressure, causes bronchodilation via β2 receptors, and induces mydriasis without cycloplegia through α1 receptor activation. It is commonly used to treat hypotension after spinal anesthesia, though selective β2 agonists are preferred for mild chronic asthma.

Adverse Effects

Common side effects include hypertension (particularly with parenteral administration), insomnia, and tachycardia. Repeated doses at short intervals may lead to tachyphylaxis (a decreased response to the drug).

Adverse Effects

Side effects may include CNS stimulation, hallucinations, and convulsions (the latter occurring primarily in cases of overdose). The typical oral dose is 10-20 mg taken twice a day, or it can be administered as an intravenous infusion of 15-60 mg in 5% glucose.

Adrenergic Antagonists

Adrenergic antagonists, also known as adrenergic blockers or sympatholytics, bind to adrenoceptors without producing the typical receptor-mediated intracellular responses. These drugs work by attaching either reversibly or irreversibly to adrenoceptors, preventing their activation by endogenous or exogenous agonists. Like adrenergic agonists, these antagonists are classified based on their relative affinity for either α or β receptors within the sympathetic nervous system.

They are divided into five categories:

- nonselective adrenergic antagonists,
- nonselective α- and β-adrenergic antagonists,
- selective α_1- and β-adrenergic antagonists.

Adrenergic antagonists play significant roles in clinical medicine, especially for managing cardiovascular disorders.

Classification of Drugs:

α-Blockers:

1. **Nonselective α-blockers:**
   - Phenoxybenzamine (irreversible)
   - Phentolamine
2. **α_1-Selective blockers:**
   - Prazosin
   - Doxazosin
   - Terazosin
   - Alfuzosin
3. **α_1A-Selective blockers:**
   - Tamsulosin
4. **α_2-Selective blockers:**
   - Yohimbine

Nonselective β_1 and β_2 Blockers (affect both β_1 and β_2 receptors):

1. Propranolol
2. Carvedilol
3. Labetalol
4. Nadolol
5. Penbutolol
6. Pindolol
7. Sotalol
8. Timolol
9. Carteolol

β_1-Selective Blockers (primarily affect β_1 receptors, also called cardioselective):

1. Atenolol
2. Metoprolol
3. Betaxolol
4. Bisoprolol
5. Celiprolol
6. Esmolol (ultra-short-acting)
7. Nebivolol (vasodilatory)
8. Acebutolol (partial agonist)

α_1 and β-Selective Blockers (block both α_1 and β receptors):

1. Labetalol
2. Carvedilol (at high concentrations, also a calcium channel blocker)

α-Adrenergic Blocking Agents

α-Adrenergic blocking agents inhibit α-adrenergic receptors (either α1 or α2), depending on their receptor subtype specificity. Drugs that block α1 receptors significantly affect blood pressure by reducing sympathetic influence on blood vessels, which lowers peripheral vascular resistance and results in decreased blood pressure. This drop often triggers reflex tachycardia, with the extent varying based on the individual's baseline sympathetic activity. Selective α2 receptor blockers have limited clinical applications.

A. Phenoxybenzamine

Phenoxybenzamine is a nonselective, irreversible, and noncompetitive blocker of both α1- and α2-adrenergic receptors. The body can counteract the blockade by synthesizing new receptors, a process that takes around a day or longer. Therefore, the effects of phenoxybenzamine persist for about 24 hours.

1. Actions:

Cardiovascular Effects: Phenoxybenzamine blocks α1-mediated vasoconstriction, reducing peripheral resistance and causing reflex tachycardia. However, it also increases norepinephrine release by blocking presynaptic α2 receptors, raising heart rate and cardiac output via β1 receptors, which may lead to arrhythmias and angina. It is ineffective for sustaining lowered blood pressure in hypertensive patients.

Epinephrine Reversal: As an α-adrenergic blocker, phenoxybenzamine counteracts epinephrine's α-agonist effects, blocking vasoconstriction while preserving β2-mediated vasodilation, resulting in decreased systemic blood pressure. Norepinephrine's effects are reduced but not fully reversed.

2. **Therapeutic Uses:** Phenoxybenzamine is indicated for managing sweating and hypertension in pheochromocytoma and may also be effective in treating Raynaud's disease and frostbite.

3. **Adverse Effects:** Phenoxybenzamine can lead to postural hypotension, nasal congestion, nausea, and vomiting. It may inhibit ejaculation and induce reflex tachycardia via the baroreceptor reflex. Caution is advised when using this medication in patients with cerebrovascular or cardiovascular diseases.

B. Prazosin, Terazosin, and Doxazosin

Prazosin, terazosin, and doxazosin are selective competitive blockers targeting the α1 receptor.

Mechanism of Action

These agents lower blood pressure and reduce peripheral vascular resistance by relaxing both arterial and venous smooth muscle. Unlike phenoxybenzamine and phentolamine, they minimally affect cardiac output, renal blood flow, and glomerular filtration rate. Tamsulosin, alfuzosin, and silodosin are more selective for α1A receptors in the prostate and bladder than for α1B receptors in blood vessels, leading to less pronounced blood pressure effects. Blocking α1A receptors decreases tone in smooth muscle at the bladder, neck, and prostate, enhancing urine flow.

Therapeutic Uses

Tolerance: None

First-Dose: Hypotension

Mitigation: Bedtime

Lipid: Improvement

Monotherapy: Not-recommended

Adverse Effects:

Dizziness, Fatigue, Nasal Congestion, Headaches, Drowsiness, Orthostatic Hypotension, Floppy Iris Syndrome

Drug Interactions: Additive effect with vasodilators (e.g., nitrates) and PDE-5 inhibitors (e.g., sildenafil)

III. β-ADRENERGIC BLOCKING AGENTS

All clinically available β-blockers are competitive antagonists. Nonselective β-blockers inhibit both β1 and β2 receptors, while cardioselective β antagonists primarily target β1 receptors; there are no clinically effective β2-selective antagonists. These drugs vary in intrinsic sympathomimetic activity, CNS effects, receptor blockade, vasodilation, and pharmacokinetics. While all β-blockers effectively lower blood pressure, they do not cause postural hypotension as α adrenoceptors remain functional. β-Blockers are used to manage systemic and portal hypertension, angina, cardiac arrhythmias, myocardial infarction, heart failure, hyperthyroidism, Glaucoma, and migraine prophylaxis.

A. Propranolol: A Nonselective β Antagonist

Propranolol serves as the prototype β-adrenergic antagonist, blocking both β1 and β2 receptors with equal affinity.

Actions:

Cardiovascular Effects: Propranolol reduces cardiac output via negative inotropic and chronotropic effects, leading to bradycardia and limiting dosage.

Peripheral Vasoconstriction: Nonselective β-blockade inhibits β2-mediated vasodilation, increasing peripheral vascular resistance. This results in lower blood pressure, which can trigger reflex peripheral vasoconstriction, reducing blood flow to the periphery.

Gradual Blood Pressure Reduction: Propranolol leads to a gradual reduction in both systolic and diastolic blood pressure through decreased cardiac output, inhibition of renal renin release, long-term reduction in total peripheral resistance, and decreased sympathetic outflow.

Bronchoconstriction: Blocking β2 receptors in the lungs can induce bronchial contraction, worsening conditions in patients with COPD or asthma, making nonselective β-blockers contraindicated in asthmatics and requiring caution in COPD patients.

Glucose Metabolism Disturbances: β-Blockade may decrease glycogenolysis and glucagon secretion, necessitating careful blood glucose monitoring in diabetic patients on insulin. β-blockers can cause pronounced hypoglycemia and blunt the physiological response to hypoglycemia, although diaphoresis during such episodes may still occur.

2. Therapeutic Uses:

- **Hypertension:** It lowers blood pressure primarily through decreased cardiac output and by inhibiting renin release from the kidneys, decreasing total peripheral resistance over time, and reducing sympathetic outflow from the CNS.
- **Angina Pectoris:** Propranolol effectively reduces the oxygen demand of the heart muscle during exertion.
- **Myocardial Infarction:** Propranolol provides protective effects on the myocardium. This protective effect may be due to reduced actions of circulating catecholamines that increase oxygen demand in an ischemic heart. Propranolol also decreases the incidence of sudden arrhythmic death following myocardial infarction.
- **Migraine:** Propranolol is effective for migraine prophylaxis, as it reduces the frequency of migraine episodes. Its lipophilic

properties allow it to penetrate the CNS, making it particularly useful for this indication.

- **Hyperthyroidism:** Propranolol and other β-blockers are beneficial in alleviating the sympathetic overstimulation associated with hyperthyroidism.

3. Pharmacokinetics:

- **Absorption:** After oral administration, propranolol is nearly completely absorbed but undergoes significant first-pass metabolism in the liver, resulting in only about 25% of the administered dose reaching the systemic circulation.
- **Volume of Distribution:** Propranolol has a large volume of distribution (approximately 4 L/kg), indicating extensive distribution into tissues.
- **Blood-Brain Barrier Penetration:** Due to its high lipophilicity, propranolol readily crosses the blood-brain barrier, which contributes to its CNS effects.
- **Metabolism and Excretion:** Propranolol is extensively metabolized in the liver, and most metabolites are excreted in the urine.

4. Adverse Effects:

a. **Bronchoconstriction:** Propranolol can cause significant bronchoconstriction by blocking β2 receptors. This effect can lead to severe respiratory distress and has been associated with fatalities in asthmatic patients who were inadvertently administered the drug. Therefore, propranolol is contraindicated in patients with COPD or asthma.

b. **Arrhythmias:** Abrupt discontinuation of β-blocker therapy can precipitate serious cardiac arrhythmias.

c. **Sexual Impairment:** Male patients taking propranolol may experience sexual impairment, the exact mechanisms of which are unclear.

d. **Metabolic Disturbances:** β-blockade can lead to decreased glycogenolysis and glucagon secretion, potentially resulting in fasting hypoglycemia.

e. **CNS Effects:** Propranolol can produce various central nervous system effects, including depression, dizziness, lethargy, fatigue, weakness, visual disturbances, hallucinations, short-term memory loss, emotional lability, and vivid dreams or nightmares.

Drug Interactions: Propranolol's metabolism can be affected by other medications that interfere with hepatic enzymes, such as cimetidine and fluoxetine.

B. Nadolol and Timolol: Nonselective β Antagonists

- **Nadolol** and **Timolol** are nonselective β-blockers that block both β1 and β2 adrenoceptors. They are considered more potent than propranolol.

Treatment of Glaucoma:

- **Mechanism of Action:** β-blockers, such as Timolol, when applied topically, effectively diminish intraocular pressure in Glaucoma by decreasing aqueous humor secretion from the ciliary body.
- **Other β-Blockers for Glaucoma:**
  - **Carteolol**, **Levobunolol**, and **Metipranolol** are nonselective β antagonists used similarly.
  - **Betaxolol** is a β1-selective agent that is also used in glaucoma management.
- **Advantages:** Unlike cholinergic drugs used in glaucoma treatment, nonselective β-blockers do not affect the eye's ability to focus on near vision or change pupil size.
- **Onset and Duration:** When administered intraocularly, the onset of action is approximately 30 minutes, with effects lasting for 12 to 24 hours.
- **Indication:** β-blockers are indicated only for the chronic management of Glaucoma. In cases of acute glaucoma attacks, **Pilocarpine** remains the drug of choice for the rapid lowering of intraocular pressure.

Summary of Glaucoma Treatments:

- **Chronic Management:** Timolol, Nadolol, carteolol, levobunolol, metipranolol, and betaxolol.
- **Acute Management:** Pilocarpine for emergency scenarios.

3.2 CHOLINERGIC AND ANTICHOLINERGIC DRUGS

1. Cholinergic Drugs:

Definition: These are the drugs that produce action similar to acetylcholine by interacting with cholinergic receptors or by increasing the acetylcholine.

Classification of Cholinergic Drugs:

1. **Choline esters:** Acetylcholine, Methacholine, Carbachol, Bethanechol
2. **Alkaloids:** Muscarine, Pilocarpine, Arecoline.
3. **Anticholinesterase:**
   a) **Reversible:** Physostigmine, Neostigmine, Pyridostigmine, Edrophonium, Tacrine, Rivastigmine
   b) **Irreversible**: Organophosphates (Malathion, Dyflos, Diazinon)

Actions:

1. **Heart:** Decrease in heart rate and cardiac output.
2. **Blood vessels:** Decrease in blood pressure: Injection of ACh causes vasodilatation
3. **Eye:** Contraction of circular muscle of the iris
4. **Smooth muscle:** Contraction in most of the organs.
5. **Additional actions:** Acetylcholine acts in the gastrointestinal (GI) system by stimulating intestinal secretions and motility, increasing gastric acid production, and increasing salivary secretion. Bronchoconstriction and increased bronchiolar secretions are among its effects.

Anticholinesterases: These are the esters of carbamic acid or the derivatives of phosphoric acid. Anti-ChE stimulates the ganglia and produces complex effects on the CVS. Lipophilic so easily penetrates into the brain and enhances cognition in Alzheimer's disease.

Pharmacokinetics: Physostigmine is absorbed rapidly across BBB, Neostigmine is absorbed slightly but does not cross BBB, and organophosphates are absorbed in all the sites of the body, like the skin and lungs. All the drugs excreted unchanged in urine.

Adverse effects: Cholinergic stimulation leads to flushing, salivation, decrease in blood pressure, Bronchospasm, abdominal pain, nausea, and diarrhea.

Interactions: Methacholine is only slightly enhanced by anticholinesterase and has additive effects when used with carbachol or bethanechol. Competitively, atropine and its derivatives oppose the Muscarinic actions.

Therapeutic uses: Choline esters are rarely used. Bethanechol has been used in postoperative urinary retention. Pilocarpine is used only in eye drops for open-angle Glaucoma. Used in the treatment of Myasthenia gravis. Used for Postoperative decurarization, particularly Neostigmine used to reverse the muscle paralysis. Used for primary treatment in Cobra bite, belladonna poisoning, and other drug overdoses like antidepressants. Anticholinesterases are used for the treatment of Alzheimer's disease as cognitive enhancers.

2. **Anticholinergic Drugs:** Drugs that block the actions of the muscarinic receptors and decrease the acetylcholine levels. Atropine is the prototype drug.

Classification of Anticholinergic Drugs:

1. **Natural alkaloids**: Atropine, Hyoscine (Scopolamine).
2. **Semisynthetic derivatives:** Homatropine, Atropine metho nitrate, Hyoscine butyl bromide, Ipratropium bromide, Tiotropium bromide.
3. **Synthetic compounds:**
   a. Mydriatics: Cyclopentolate, Tropicamide
   b. Antisecretory-anti spasmodics:
   i) Quaternary compounds: propantheli, Oxyphenonium, Clidinium, Pipenzol, methyl bromide, Isopropamide, and Glycoprolate.
   ii) Tertiary amines: Dicyclomine, Valethama, Pirenzepine.
   c. Vasicoselective: Oxybutynin, Flavoxa:.Tolterodine.
   d. Antiparkinsonian: Trihexyphenidyl (Benzhxol), Procyclidine, Biperiden.

Actions:

1. **CNS:** Atropine produces the CNS stimulant effect. Atropine stimulates many medullary centers —vagal, respiratory, and vasomotor.
2. **CVS:** Prominently, atropine produces the tachycardia. No effect on the blood vessels
3. **Eye:** On iris muscles produce mydriasis. Intraocular tension rises.
4. **Smooth muscles:** Contraction of the stomach and small intestine is reduced by atropine. Spasms and constipation are relieved
5. **Glands:** Decrease in gland secretions, eyes dryness, decrease in sweat, salivary and lacrimal secretions.
6. **Body Temperature:** Increase in body temperature due to a decrease in sweat secretions.
7. **Local anesthetic:** Mild local anesthetic action produced on the eye.

Pharmacokinetics: Atropine is well absorbed after administration in several routes. Absorbed in the eye and slightly absorbed in BBB.

Metabolised in the liver by hydrolysis and conjugation, excreted unchanged in urine.

Adverse Effects: Dry mouth, difficulty in swallowing and talking. Ataxia, delirium, hypotension, excitement, cardiovascular collapse, and respiratory depression.

Drug Interactions: Atropine delays the gastric emptying of drugs and slows the absorption of drugs. Antacids interfere with the absorption of anticholinergics. Antihistamines, tricyclic antidepressants, and phenithiazines have additive effects with anticholinergics.

Therapeutic uses: Used as **anti-secretary action** in pre-anesthetic medication, used to decrease gastric acid secretions in peptic ulcers and reduce pulmonary secretions in pulmonary embolism. As **anti-spasmodic action** used in relieving abdominal cramps, spastic constipation and gastritis. Useful for relieving urinary urgency and frequency. In bronchial asthma COPD, a decrease in secretions and bronchodilator action produces relief in asthma patients. Frequently used as a cycloplegia and mydriatic agent. Atropine is used in counteracting the partial heart block. Anti Muscarinic agents are used in the treatment of Parkinson's disease motion sickness and to antagonize muscarinic overdose or poisoning.

3.3 NEUROMUSCULAR BLOCKING AGENTS

Introduction

There is a need for skeletal muscle relaxants to facilitate surgery. Hence, these drugs are used along with surgical anesthesia. They relax skeletal muscles, particularly the abdominal wall and lower limbs, so that operative manipulations become easier. This situation minimizes the risk of respiratory and cardiovascular depression and reduces the post-anesthetic recovery period because, in the presence of skeletal muscle relaxants, lighter anesthesia is sufficient. The drugs block post-synaptic actions of ACh at the motor end plate. Some muscle relaxants simply reduce spasticity in a few painful conditions like chronic back pain and myalgia. Based on their site and mechanism of action, skeletal muscle relaxants are broadly classified as neuromuscular blocking agents and peripheral muscle relaxants.

Neuromuscular Blocking Agents

Whenever a nerve joins a muscle, there is no anatomical continuity between them. There is a small gap between a nerve and a muscle. It is called the neuromuscular junction (NMJ). These drugs act at NMJ. At

NMJ, ACh works as a neurotransmitter through nicotinic receptors. Hence, drugs blocking nicotinic actions of ACh perform as neuromuscular blocking agents.

They are sub-classified into two sub-categories:

1. Non-depolarising blockers (competitive blockers) and
2. Depolarising blockers (persistent depolarisers).

1. **Non-Depolarising Blockers (Competitive Blockers):** The first NMJ blocker was curare, which native hunters of South America used for paralysing an animal before hunting. Curare was a plant extract, and d-Tubocurarine (d-TC) was isolated and used in clinical practice from the 1940s. There are several derivatives of d-TC. Some are long-acting, e.g., Metocurine, Doxacurium, Pancuronium, and Pipecuronium, and some others are short-acting, e.g., Atracurium, Cis-atracurium, Mivacurium, Vecuronium, Rocuronium and Rapacuronium.

Mechanism of Action

d-TC and other non-depolarising blockers are quaternary compounds with two positively charged nitrogen in their structure. (see Fig. 3.19). These drugs have an affinity for NM cholinergic receptors at the motor end plate but have no intrinsic activity over them. They block the NM receptor and prevent the binding of ACh to the site. As a result, the necessary conformational change in the NM receptor needed for opening the sodium channel is prevented. In the absence of end plate potential, the motor nerve impulses cannot induce contractions in the skeletal muscle. The net result is the relaxation of skeletal muscles. They do not cause depolarisation by themselves but prevent depolarisation by ACh. The antagonism is competitive in nature. Anticholinesterase drugs like Physostigmin/ Neostigmincan can reverse the NMJ block due to an increase in the concentration of ACh. At higher concentrations, these drugs block sodium channels directly, which adds to the strength of the blockade. This leads to further weakening of NMJ transmission and reduces the ability of drugs like Physostigmin/ Neostigmin to reverse the actions of non-depolarising muscle relaxants.

Pharmacokinetics

- These drugs are not absorbed when given orally. They are given intravenously but differ in potency, rate of onset, and duration of action.
- They have a relatively small volume of distribution (Vd). None of them cross the brain barrier. Hence, they do not produce CNS toxicity.

- These drugs do not cross the placental barrier and hence do not affect the newborn if used during cesarean section.
- The route of elimination controls the duration of action. Drugs excreted by the kidney have a longer duration of action. Drugs eliminated by the liver have an intermediate
- duration of action, and drugs inactivated by plasma cholinesterase have a shorter duration of action.
- Steroidal NMJ blockers (Vecuronium, Rocoronium, and Rapacuronium) may show accumulation and cause prolonged paralysis.
- Artracurium is chemically unstable at alkaline pH and has a shorter duration of action during respiratory alkalosis caused by hyperventilation.
- There is no pharmacogenetic variation in metabolism in the case of these drugs.

Pharmacodynamics

- After intravenous injections of d-TC-like drugs, motor weakness gives way to progressive flaccid paralysis. The fast-moving smaller muscles like those of the eyes, jaw, toes, and larynx are affected initially. Larger muscles like that of limbs and trunk are affected next. Finally, the intercostal muscles and the diaphragm are paralyzed. Recovery of muscles usually occurs in the reverse order.
- Some derivatives of d-TC have a tendency to liberate histamine from mast cells. Steroidal derivatives of d-TC like Pancuronium, Vecuronium, Pipecuronium, Rocuronium, and Rapacuronium cause the least histamine release.
- At common clinical doses, d-TC and Metocurine exhibit partial blockade of autonomic ganglia. Other derivatives like Doxacurium, Mivacurium, Atracurium, and cis-atracurium exhibit the least blockade. Steroidal derivatives do not block autonomic ganglia.
- Only Pancuronium has vagolytic action due to the blockade of M2 receptors leading to tachycardia. Other drugs are devoid of vagolytic action.
- d-TC and drugs like Metocurine, Mevacurium, and Atracurium produce hypotension partly due to histamine release and partly due to ganglionic blockade. Only Pancuronium causes tachycardia; other drugs do not.
- Only d-TC can cause broncho-spasm due to the release of histamine from mast cells.

- d-TC like drugs decrease the tone and motility of GIT. Recovery is followed by constipation.

Reversal of Blockade

Neostigmine and Pyridostigmine antagonise or reverse the non-depolarising neuromuscular blockade caused by d-TC like drugs. The effect is due to an increase in the concentration of ACh at the motor end plate. Reversal of the blockade becomes necessary if long-acting or intermediate-acting d-TC like drugs are used. Short-acting drugs do not need such reversal.

Adverse Effects

- These are related to skeletal muscle paralysis, histamine release, ganglionic blockade, or vagolytic actions.
- Hypoxia and respiratory paralysis may be caused by d-TC like drugs. It may be accompanied by Bronchospasm, hypotension, and bradycardia.
- Pancuronium may cause tachycardia.

Synergists and Antagonists

- Anticholinesterases like Neostigmine are antagonists to non-depolarising neuromuscular blockade caused by d-TC like drugs.
- Hypothermia enhances the depolarising action of ACh. Hence, it antagonizes the action of non-depolarising blockers.
- Inhalational general anesthetics like Halothane decrease the sensitivity of postjunctional membrane to depolarisation and, therefore, act synergistically with d-TC like drugs. Hence, their doses should be reduced when used along with inhalational anesthetics.
- Aminoglycoside antibiotics like Gentamycin cause neuromuscular blockade by decreasing ACh release. Other antibiotics like Polymyxin-B, Clindamycin, Lincomycin and Tetracycline group of antibiotics may also cause neuromuscular blockade. All these drugs can act synergistically when used with d-TC like drugs.
- In large doses, most local anesthetics block neuromuscular transmission and can act synergistically with d-TC like drugs. Other drugs like Quinidine, Propranolol, Diltiazem, Digitalis, Diuretics, and Chloroquinine can also show synergism with d- TC-like drugs.
- Myasthenia gravis markedly adds to neuromuscular blockade caused by d-TC like drugs. Conversely, patients with burns and those with upper motor neuron disease require larger doses of d-TC-like drugs.

- Atracurium: ATRELAX TRACRIUIM is available as an injection of 10 mg/ml.
- *Pancuronium*: PANCURONIUM BROMIDE, PANCONIUM is available as 2 mg/ml injection.
- *Pipecuronium*: ARDUAN is available as 4 mg/2 ml injection. Recuronium: CUROMID is available as 50 mg/ml injection, and Vecuronium: VERUNIUM, VECURON is available as 10 mg/2 ml or 4 mg/2 ml injection.

2. Depolarising Blockers (Persistent Depolarisers): Succinyl Choline (Sch)

Only one depolarising neuromuscular blocker is available in clinical practice. It is Succinylcholine (SCh). The actions of SCh are detailed below;

Mechanism of Action

SCh is an analog of ACh. SCh is hydrolyzed by pseudocholinesterase but not by true AChE. As a result, only a small intravenous dose of SCh reaches NMJ after being hydrolyzed by pseudocholinesterase. At NMJ, it acts like an excess of ACh, and its actions persist for a longer duration because it is not degraded by true AChE. SCh reacts with NM receptors of the motor end plate, opening up sodium channel and causing depolarisation, which then spreads and causes repetitive excitation of muscle motor units leading to transient muscle fasciculations. Effectively, SCh continues to keep muscles next to NMJ in a polarized state. The action results in flaccid paralysis, which cannot be reversed by AChE inhibitors like Neostigmine. This is called the phase I block. With higher doses of SCh or its prolonged infusion, phase I block can get converted in to a non-depolarising type phase II block. The phase II block resembles that of d-TC and can be reversed by Neostigmine. Conversion from phase I to phase II is slow. During long surgeries, d-TC like drugs are preferred over SCh because of the uncertainty of phase I/phase II in the case of SCh. Only during short operative procedures SCh is preferred because of muscle relaxation in phase I.

Pharmacokinetics

SCh possesses two quaternary groups in its structure. It is not absorbed if given orally and does not cross the bold-brain barrier or placental barrier. It is administered intravenously in a dose of 0.75-1.5 mg/kg. The duration of action is very short (5-10 minutes). It is primarily due to hydrolysis by pseudocholinesterase present in plasma. Its action is terminated by its diffusion from the motor end plate to extra-cellular fluid. NMJ blockade by SCh may be prolonged in patients with genetic variation having atypical pseudocholinesterase. The ability of the enzyme pseudocholinesterase to metabolize SCh is expressed as a "dibucaine number". For a normal person, the dibucaine number is 80, and a number less than 80 indicates a proportionate concentration of atypical enzyme.

Pharmacodynamics

After a single intravenous dose of SCh, fasciculations over the chest and abdomen occur briefly. Complete relaxation occurs within 1-2 minutes and disappears within 5-10 minutes. Twitches on the cheek and abdomen appear first. Paralysis then spreads to the neck, limbs, face, trunk, and then to respiratory muscles. The onset and recovery are rapid, and the sequence of paralysis is not distinguishable.

SCh stimulates ganglia due to agonistic action on the NN receptor. Histamine release is less than that of d-TC. Initial bradycardia due to stimulation of the vagal ganglia is followed by tachycardia and hypertension due to stimulation of the sympathetic ganglia. However, blood pressure is not affected much due to vasodilatation caused by muscarinic actions.

Adverse Effects

- **Hyperkalaemia:** Efflux of potassium leads to hyperkalaemia. In susceptible patients, like cases of burns, spinal injury, and uraemia, hyperkalaemia can precipitate arrhythmia or cardiac arrest.
- **Malignant hyperthermia:** It is a genetically inherited condition caused by mutation of calcium-releasing channels of the sarcoplasmic reticulum. In susceptible individuals, persistent release of calcium leads to persistent muscle contraction and increased heat production due to skeletal muscle contraction. The condition may be aggravated if general anaesthetics like Halothane are used along with SCh.
- **Muscle rigidity:** It is yet another genetic abnormality caused by a mutation of voltage-sensitive sodium channels. In such individuals, SCh may complicate endotracheal tube insertion.
- **Prolonged apnoea:** Persons with atypical pseudocholinesterase show prolonged apnoea. Increased intra-gastric pressure Nausea and vomiting with SCh occur due to an increase in intra-gastric pressure as a consequence of fasciculations.
- **Rise in intra-occular pressure:** The rise in intra-occular pressure is only for a short while (5-10 minutes). It occurs due to contractions of myofibrils and partly due to transient dilatation of related blood vessels.

- **Muscle soreness:** Some patients show myoglobinuria following the use of SCh. Hence, muscle soreness after recovery is a common observation in such patients.

Synergists and antagonists

- Neostigmine potentiates phase I block caused by SCh.
- Hypothermia potentiates the action of SCh.
- Calcium channel blockers like Verapamil or Diltiazem enhance NMJ blockade caused by SCh.
- Duration of action as well as toxicity of SCh increases in infants below 1 year, patients with collagen disease, thyrotoxicosis and in patients with atypical pseudocholinesterase.
- SCh is available as injections of 50 mg/ml: SCOLINE, ENTUBATE, MIDARINE.

Therapeutic Uses of NMJ Blockers

Adjuvant to general anaesthesia: All NMJ blockers (d-TC like drugs and SCh) are used to provide skeletal muscle relaxation during abdominal or thoracic surgery and for endotracheal intubation. They are also used to counteract laryngospasm during barbiturate anaesthesia. They are also used to prevent muscle contractions during surgery. SCh is preferred for brief procedures. For relatively long-term use, d-TC like drugs are preferred based on their pharmacokinetics.

To prevent trauma during electro-convulsive therapy (ECT): SCh with Diazepam is used to prevent injuries or fractures due to excessive convulsions caused by ECT. The combination can also be used for the reduction of fractures and other orthopaedic surgeries.

In different spastic conditions: In spastic conditions like tetanus or status epilepticus, NMJ blockers are used when Diazepam alone is not sufficient.

To control ventilation: In patients with obstructive airway disease, NMJ blockers eliminate chest wall resistance and eliminate ineffective spontaneous ventilation.

3.4 DRUGS USED IN MYASTHENIA GRAVIS

Etiology and Symptoms

- Myasthenia gravis is an acquired auto-immune disorder causing fatigue and weakness of skeletal muscles.

- The disease is associated with the production of IgG-type antibodies to ACh receptors (NM) at the post-junctional motor end plate.
- In 90% of patients having this disease, the anti-ACh antibody titre is raised.
- Reduction in the number of NM receptors results in the reduction in the end plate potential amplitude, which in turn fails to trigger an action potential.

The ***symptoms*** *include*:

The weakness of muscle and fatigue worsens after exercise but goes off after rest. The weakness in muscles is not associated with pain. In the early stages of the disease, the fast-moving muscles are affected first. Hence, symptoms start with ptosis, diplopia, slurring of speech, difficulty in swallowing, and weakness of extremities. Subsequently, all muscles are progressively affected including respiratory muscles. The thymus shows abnormality in about 75% of cases of myasthenia gravis.

Treatment of Myasthenia Gravis

Any reversible anti-AChE drug of an intermediate duration of action is useful for the treatment of myasthenia gravis. Initially, the doses are given on an empirical basis but later titrated for prolonged therapy.

Initially, **Neostigmine** is given in an oral dose of 15-30 mg/day in divided doses or 0.5-2.5 mg as intramuscular or subcutaneous injection with gradual increments till therapeutic goals are achieved. Alternatively, oral **Pyridostigmine** 60 mg three times a day is followed by a gradual increase till satisfactory response. Another alternative is oral Ambenonium 2.5-5 mg every 6 hours.

Sustained release preparations of Pyridostigmine are also available, which can be given at bed time. **Longer-acting AChEinihibitors** like organophosphates are not used. During prolonged therapy, titration of the dose is done. The patient's condition may swing between myasthenia gravis (due to lower doses of drugs) or cholinergic crisis (due to toxicity of drugs). Both conditions can end up into muscular weakness. In such cases, doses of anti-AChE drugs need to be adjusted. Prior to such dose adjustments, **Edrophonium** is given intravenously in a dose of 2 mg. If the condition worsens due to Edrophonium, the muscular weakness is due to overdosing on an AChE dose like Neostigmine. On the contrary, if the condition of the patient improves after the Edrophonium dose, the muscle weakness is due to myasthenia gravis. Based on the response to Edrophonium, the dose of the anti-AChE drug is adjusted.

Drugs-induced Myasthenia Gravis

The following drugs are known to aggravate myasthenia gravis. Doses of these drugs should be reduced, or these drugs may be withdrawn during treatment of myasthenia gravis.

Drugs that aggravate myasthenia gravis

S. No.	Category of drug	Examples
1.	Antibiotics	Aminoglycosides Polymixins, Colistin (Streptomycin, Gentamycin),
2.	Antiarrhythmics	Procainamide, Quinidine and Propranolol
3.	CNS depressants	Morphine (respiratory depression)
4.	Miscellaneous	d-TC, Quinine, Methoxyflurane and Lithium

Since the etiology of myasthenia gravis originates in auto-immunity, drugs like glucocorticoids (Prednisolone) and immune-suppressants (Azathioprine, Cyclosporine) are used to treat myasthenia gravis. In addition, techniques like thymectomy or plasmapheresis are also used to treat myasthenia gravis.

CHAPTER 4

Neurohumoral Transmission in CNS

Neurohumoral transmission refers to the process by which nerve cells, also known as neurons, communicate with other cells in the body, such as muscle cells or other neurons, through the release of chemical neurotransmitters called hormones.

4.1 MAJOR NEUROTRANSMITTERS IN CNS AND THEIR FUNCTIONS

Small Molecules

Biogenic Amines

- Serotonin
- Dopamine
- Histamine
- Epinephrine
- Norepinephrine

Amino acids

- Glutamate
- Aspartate
- GABA
- Glycine

Others

- Acetylcholine
- Nitric oxide

Neuromodulators

- Neuropeptide-y
- Substance-p

Lipid Mediators

- Prostaglandins

Growth factors

- Nerve growth factor
- Brain-derived growth factor

Properties of Neurotransmitters

- Synthesized in the presynaptic neuron
- Localized to vesicles in the presynaptic neuron
- Released from the presynaptic neuron under physiological condition
- Rapidly removed from the synaptic cleft by uptake or degradation
- Presence of receptor on the postsynaptic neuron.
- Binding to the receptor elicits a biological response

Process of Neurohumoral Transmission

When a neuron receives a signal, it generates an electrical impulse that travels down its axon to the end of the neuron called the axon terminal. At the axon terminal, the electrical impulse triggers the release of neurotransmitters, which then diffuse across a tiny gap called the synaptic bond to specific receptors on the target cell. Triggers a series of chemical and electrical events in the target cell lead to the desired response (such as muscle contraction or the initiation of a new electrical impulse in a neighbouring neuron).

Main Neurotransmitter in the CNS are

Amino acid Neurotransmitters

- GABA (Inhibitory Neurotransmitter)
- Glycine (Inhibitory Neurotransmitter)
- Glutamate (Excitatory Neurotransmitter)

Monoamine neurotransmitters

- Dopamine (Inhibitory Neurotransmitter)
- Serotonin (Inhibitory Neurotransmitter)
- Histamine (Excitatory Neurotransmitter)

4.2 TYPES OF NEURORECEPTORS AND THEIR FUNCTIONS

Gamma-Aminobutyric Acid (GABA)

Role of GABA in Neurohumoral Transmission

Gamma-aminobutyric acid (GABA)is an inhibitory neurotransmitter. When released by neurons, GABA binds to specific receptors on the target cell, causing an influx of negatively charged ions (such as chloride ions) into the cell, which makes the target cell less likely to generate an electrical impulse.

GABA Synthesis

Gaba is the main inhibitory Neurotransmitter in the CNS, Synthesized in the Brain. It acts by binding to specific receptors on both Pre and postsynaptic synaptic membranes. Synapses using GABA are referred to as GABAergic synapses. Glutamate Synthesized from the amino acid L-glutamic acid in the presence of GAD. Glutamic acid decarboxylase (GAD) is present in neurons, pancreatic cellsand in body fluid.GAD acts as a catalyst that removes the carboxyl group from Glutamate and produce GABA.

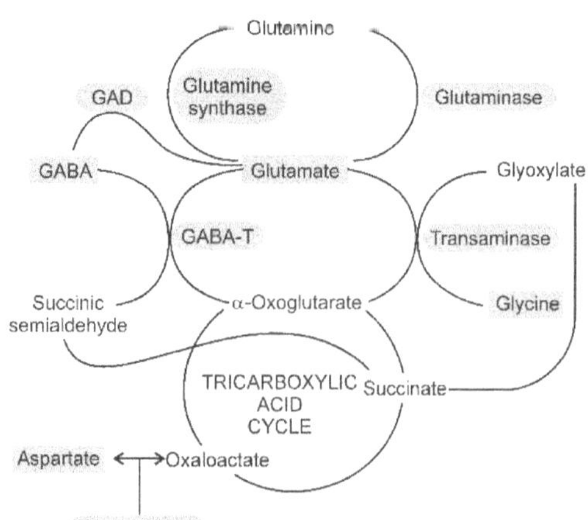

GABA Synthesis

GABA Synthesis

Storage and Release

Newly synthesized GABA is stored in synaptic vesicle by means of vesicular transporter. These are stored at the postsynaptic terminal until action potential release. Stored GABA released into the synaptic cleft is stimulated by the depolarisation of presynaptic neurons. GABA diffuses across the cleft to target receptors on the postsynaptic surface. The action of GABA is terminated by reuptake of GABA by presynaptic nerve terminals & glial cells.

GABA Synthesis

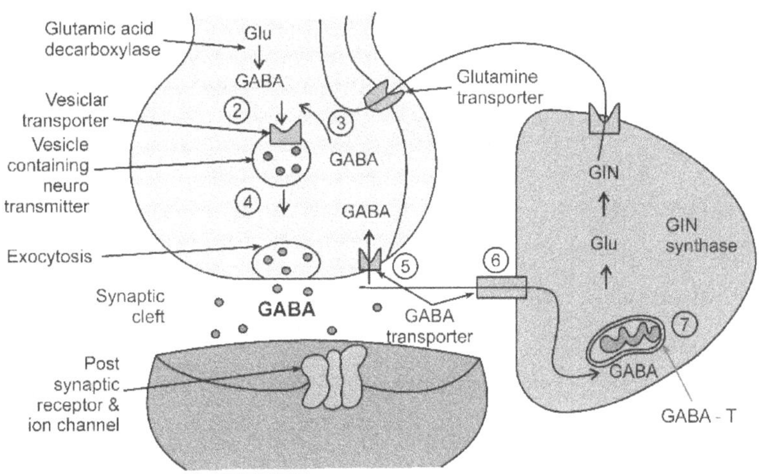

Storage Release and metabolism of GABA

Role of GABA

It is involved in the regulation of muscle tone, sleep, and anxiety. In addition, GABA is also involved in the regulation of other neurotransmitter systems, including Dopamine and serotonin.

Abnormalities of GABA Function

It has been linked to a variety of neurological and psychological disorders like epilepsy, anxiety disorders, and schizophrenia.

GABA Receptors

There are two types of GABA receptors

- GABA-A Receptors
- GABA-B Receptors

Structure of GABA$_A$ Receptor

Transmembrane pentameric receptor. Five subunits around the central pore consist of 2α,2β, and 1γ gamma subunits.

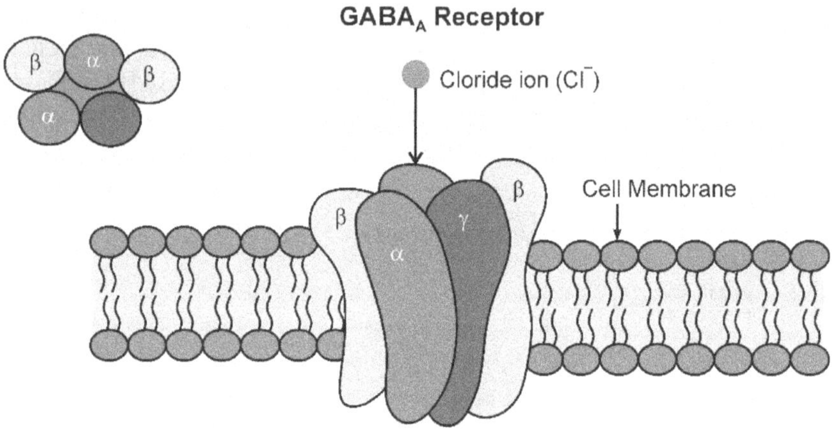

GABA$_A$ Receptor

Type: Ligand-gated ion channel Receptor

Location: GABAergic neurons

GABA$_B$ Receptor

Type: G-protein coupled receptor (GPCR)

Location: Pre & postsynaptic neurons

Glutamate

This is an Excitatory Amino Acid. Principle excitatory Neurotransmitter in CNS, stored in Neuronal cell membrane. Glutamate comes into the CNS mainly by glial cells and by Kreb's Cycle.

Role of Glutamate

Responsible for neural communication, memory formation, learning, and regulation of mood and behaviour.

Synthesis

Glutamate Comes from glial cells in the neuron. In the neurons, glutamine is converted into glutaminase with the help of the glutaminase enzyme, which stores Glutamate in the synaptic vesicles. From synaptic vesicles, glutamate is released by the process of exocytosis, which is Cat dependent.

Glutamate binds to specific receptors on the target cells, causing an influx of positively charged ions (such as sodium and calcium ions) into the cell, which makes the target cell generate more electrical impulse

Glutamate Synthesis

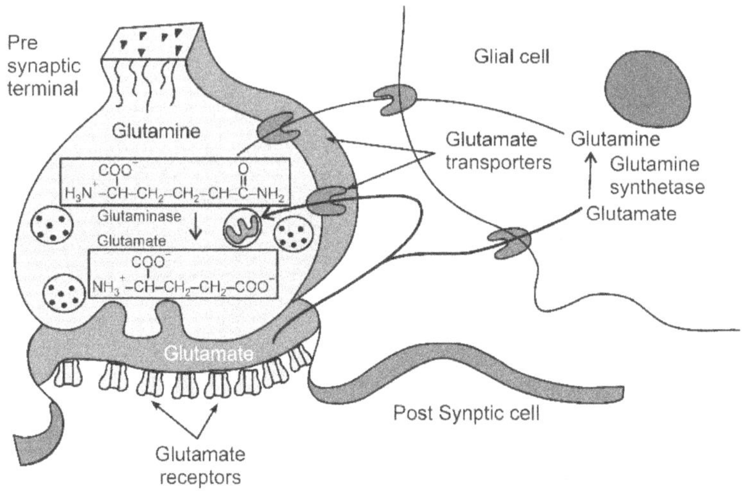

Glutamate Synthesis

In the neuronal presynaptic reuptake pump (EAAT or excitatory amino acid transporter), Glutamate is transported across membranes of synapse by these Na+ dependent transporters. These EAATIs are involved in the reuptake and release of Glutamate during glutamine cycle

The vesicular transporter for Glutamate into synaptic vesicles (vGluT).

Glutamate Receptors

Glutamate receptors are synaptic receptors located primarily on the membranes of Neuronal cells. Glutamate (glutamic acid) is abundant in the human body, particularly the nervous system, and especially prominent in the human brain where it is the body's most prominent neurotransmitter, the Brain's main inhibitory neurotransmitter. Glutamate receptors are responsible for the glutamate-mediated postsynaptic excitation of neural cells and are important for neural communication, memory formation, learning, and regulation.

Types of Glutamate receptors

- Inotropic glutamate Receptors
    - NMDA receptors
    - AMPA receptors
    - Kainate receptors
- Metabotropic glutamate Receptors

NMDA Receptors

Type: Ligand-gated ion channel Receptor

Location: Post synaptic glial cell

Function: Synaptic plasticity, Excitotoxicity

AMPA Receptors

Type: Ligand-gated ion channel Receptor

Location: Post synaptic glial cell

Function: Fast epsp

Kainate Receptors

Type: Ligand-gated ion channel Receptor

Location: Pre & postsynaptic neurons

Function: Fast epsp, Presynaptic inhibition

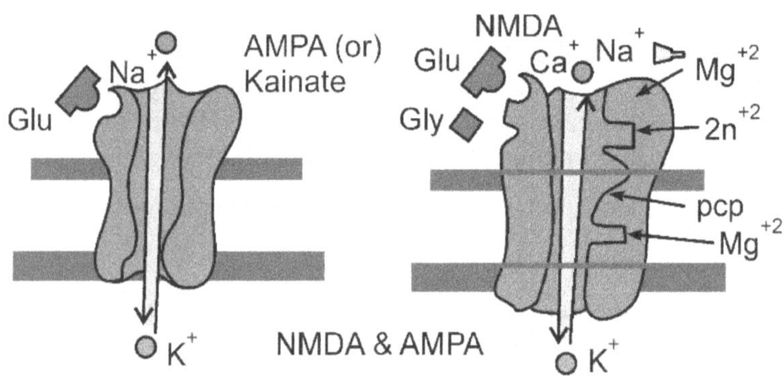

NMDA & AMPA Receptors

Metabotropic glutamate Receptors

Type: GPCR Receptor

Location: Somatodendritic & Nerveterminal

Abnormalities of Glutamate function

Excessive activation of glutamate receptors can be harmful to neurons contribute to a variety of neurological disorders, stroke, traumatic brain injury, and neurodegenerative diseases such as Alzheimer's and Parkinson's. Glutamate is also involved in the regulation of the hypothalamic-pituitary-adrenal (HPA) axis. It is involved in the body's response to stress.

Glycine

Simplest Amino acid, semi-essential Amino acid. The major Inhibitory Neurotransmitter in CNS is also known as Inhibitory chloride Channel Protein. They are present in abundance in the Spinal cord. The glycine receptor is a member of the Nicotinic receptor superfamily. Glycine binds to specific receptors on the target cell, causing an influx of negatively charged ions (such as chloride ions) into the cell, which generates an electrical impulse in the target cell. Glycine is mainly found in the Spinal Cord, and neurons in the brain stem play a key role in the regulation of reflexes, sensory procession, and the control of muscle tone.

Glycine Receptors

Type: Ligand-gated ion channel Receptor

Location: Postsynaptic, mainly in the Brain stem & spinal cord

Abnormalities of Glycine

It is particularly important for regulating the activity of motor neurons that control muscle contraction, and abnormalities in glycine function lead to a variety of neurological disorders, including hyperekplexia. Glycine is also involved in the regulation of pain perception, particularly in the spinal cord. Inhibiting glycine release in the spinal cord can enhance pain sensitivity.

Serotonin

The scientific name for serotonin is 5-hydroxytryptamine, or 5-HT. It is a monoamine neurotransmitter. About 90% of it is found/localized in the intestines, while the rest is found in the brain and platelets. The level of 5-HT in whole blood is in the range of 65250 mg/ml. It is popularly thought to be a contributor to feelings of well-being and happiness. It is a key mediator in the physiology of mood, vascular function, and gastrointestinal motility. This explains the number of therapeutic agents that act targeting the serotonergic system such as 5-HT3 antagonists, SSRIs, and triptan.

Synthesis

Serotonin is synthesized from the amino acid L- tryptophan by a short metabolic pathway consisting of the enzyme tryptophan hydroxylase (TPH).

Metabolism

Serotonin is metabolised by monoaminoxidase (MAO) to 5HT indole acetic acid (HIAA). Majorly serotonin reuptake by serotonin reuptake transporters.

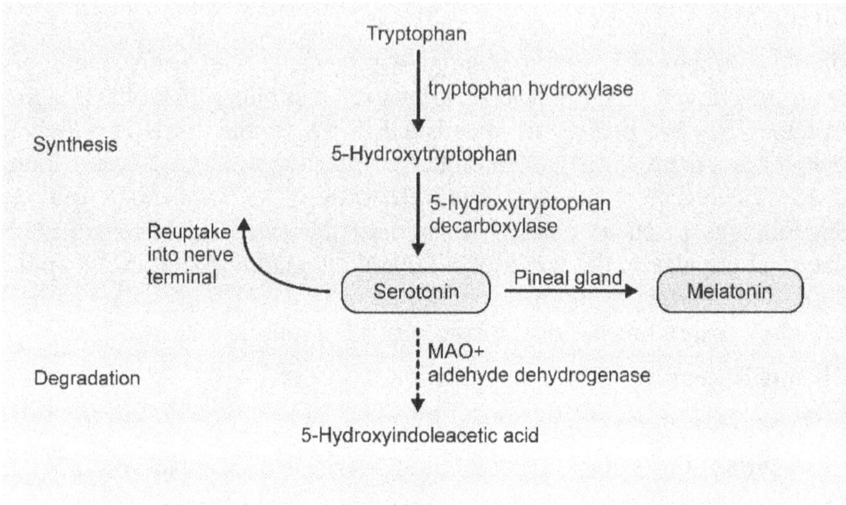

Serotonin Synthesis and metabolism

Serotonin Receptors

There are four types of 5HT receptors

- **5HT1**
  Type: GPCR Receptor
  Location: CNS, Vascular smooth, Blood vessels, Uterus, heart, GIT
- **5HT2**
  Type: GPCR Receptor
  Location: CNS, PNS, Smooth muscles, Gastric fundus
- **5HT3**
  Type: Ligand-gated ion channel Receptor
  Location: PNS, CNS
- **5HT4**
  Type: GPCR
  Location: GIT

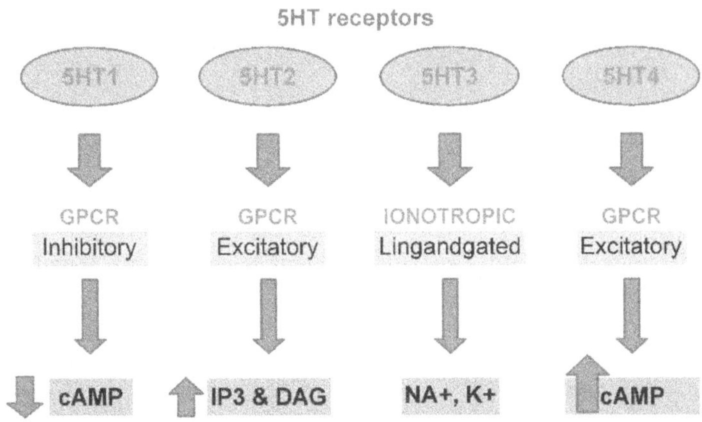

Functions of serotonin

Serotonin regulates gastrointestinal motility, mood, appetite, sleep, and some cognitive functions (memory, learning). It is one of the important neurotransmitters in the body, acting through serotonergic neurons.

Abnormalities of serotonin

In the Brain, serotonin is particularly important for regulating mood and behaviour. Abnormalities in serotonin function have been implicated in a variety of psychiatric disorders, depression, and anxiety. And schizophrenia.

Dopamine

Dopamine belongs to the family of catecholamines Hormones Epinephrine and Norepinephrine (other catecholamines) are derived from Dopamine a significant role in learning, goal-directed behaviour, and regulation of hormone motor control. Dopamine is converted from dopa. Dopamine is metabolised by MAO (Moo amino oxidase) and COMT (Catechol ortho methyltransferase)

Dopamine Receptors

There are two types Dopamine of receptors

- **D1-Like Family**

  Type: GPCR Receptor

  Location: Hippocampus

- **D2-Like Family**

  Type: GPCR Receptor

  Location: Substantia Nigra

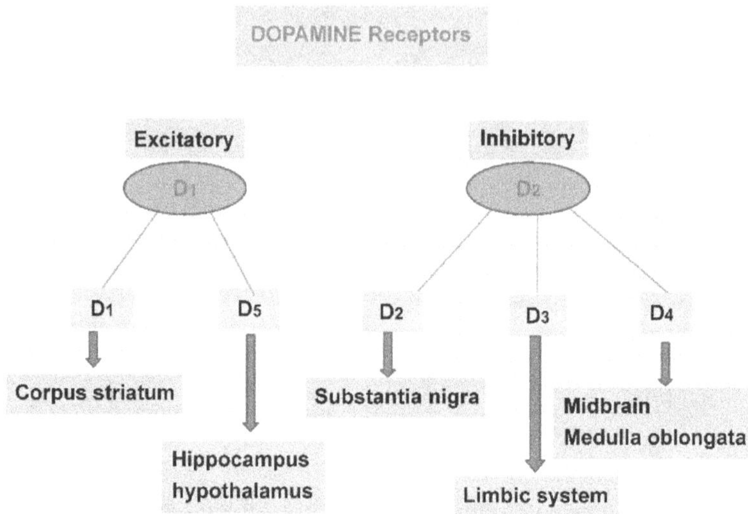

Abnormalities in Dopamine

Abnormalities in dopamine function have been implicated in a variety of neurological and psychiatric disorders, including Parkinson's disease, schizophrenia, addiction, and attention deficit hyperactivity disorder (ADHD).

CHAPTER 5

Drug Targets in the Central Nervous System (CNS)

5.1 ION CHANNELS AND NEURONAL EXCITABILITY

Ion channels and the drug-discovery process have always been connected. Their types, most commonly identified as Na+, K+, Ca2+, and Cl, have essentially been linked to processes in neurons. Consequently, medications that target them have an impact on all organs or systems that are connected to neuronal activity: the central nervous system

Voltage-gated Sodium Channels

In order to provide sodium ions with selective permeability, the voltage-gated sodium channels (VGSCs), which are heteromeric transmembrane proteins, open in response to changes in membrane potential.

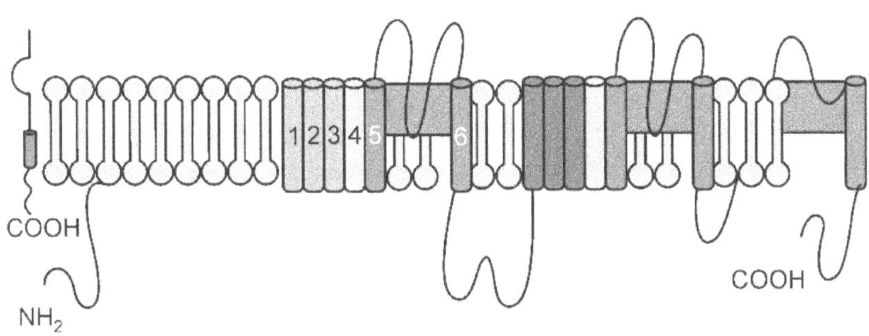

SODIUM CHANNELS

Sodium Channels

Several subunits combine to form sodium channels. A Na+-selective pore is formed by subunit beta. Its molecular weight is 260 kDa. Each of its four homologous domains (I-IV or D1-D4) has six α-helical transmembrane segments (S1-S6) and one very short, non-helical reentrant segment (SS1/SS2), sometimes referred to as the P-segment, which is situated between S5 and S6.

Sodium channels also possess one or more β-subunits of about 35 kDa. The role of β-subunits is influencing the properties of α-subunits, including modulation of sodium currents. Epilepsy is one of the most common neurological disorders. In general, there is a tendency to the occurrence of unprovoked epileptic seizures, which are a result of synchronous discharges of a large number of neurons. It is now known that abnormal expression or function of VGSCs may be involved in the pathophysiology of both acquired and inherited epilepsy. Several sodium channel blockers have been implicated in the therapy of migraine; however, their precise mechanism of action in that condition is not fully understood. Voltage-gated sodium channels located in peripheral sensory neurons play an important role in the pathophysiology of neuropathic pain. Ataxia is another condition associated with sodium channels.

Voltage-gated Potassium Channels

Voltage-gated potassium channels (VGKCs, KV) belong to the broad family of potassium channels, which all contribute to the excitability of neurons, signaling in the nervous system as well as ion homeostasis. Potassium ion channels play a critical role in the repolarization of action potentials and regulation of firing frequency. Four transmembrane pore-forming voltage-sensing α-subunits are found in voltage-gated potassium channels. The KV channel's individual α-subunit is made up of six segments (S1-S6). Multiple positive charges are carried by the four transmembrane S4 segments, which serve as the primary voltage-sensing element. The channel's shape changes in response to variations in the membrane potential. Cytoplasmic and transmembrane auxiliary β-subunits are present in native neuronal potassium channel complexes.

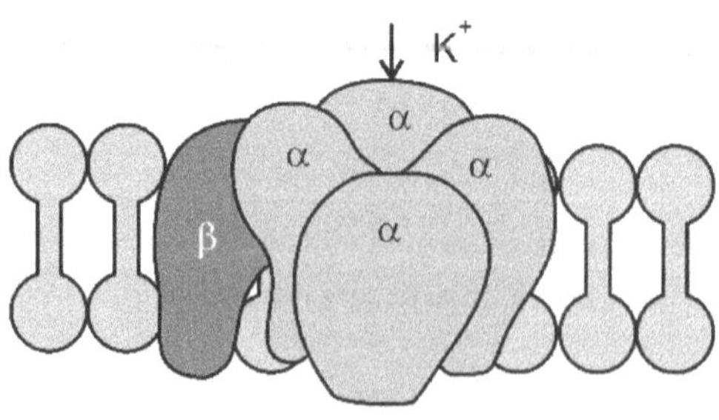

K^+ Channels

K+ channel

Voltage-gated potassium channels, because of their contribution to the excitability of neurons, may serve as drug targets in epilepsy. These channels may represent a potential target for the treatment of psychosis.

Calcium Channels

Calcium channels have been well-known drug targets, and still, they are the subject of intensive research. Voltage-gated calcium channels are present in membranes of excitable cells. They are opened during depolarization and this gives rise to an influx of Ca2+. The two families of calcium channels are called HVA (High Voltage-Activated) and LVA (Low Voltage-Activated). The HVA family includes channels of the L-, N-, P-, Q-, and R types. They are α2-δ, β, and α subunit heterotrimers. Subunit α and ancillary subunit β create a pore. By joining forces with subunit α, subunit α2-δ creates a functioning pore. The T-type channels in the LVA family are monomers made up solely of the subunit α. In CNS, they are responsible for the process of dreaming, and their mutation leads to the appearance of absence epilepsy.

Neuronal Excitability

Neuronal excitability refers to the ability of neurons to generate a large change in membrane voltage in response to a very small stimulus. This phenomenon is completely based on Action potential that is generated during nerve impulses.

Basic Principles of Nerve Impulse & Functions of Neurons

A. **Dendrites**: Receive information.

B. **Cell body**: Process & integrate information.

C. **Axon**: Carry information to long distances.

D. **Axon terminals**: Transmit information to the next neuron.

Action potential: If nerve signal stimulation is strong enough, it passes all over the neuron, this is known as action potential.

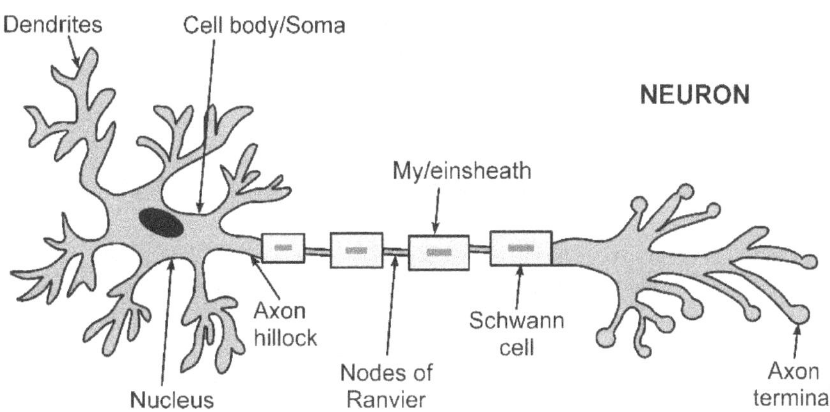

Transmission of Neuronal Signal

This process entirely depends on the movement of ions (or) charged particles.

Ions involved are:

- Na^+ - sodium (positively charged)
- K^+ - potassium (positively charged)
- Cl^- - chloride (negatively charged)

These ions distribution is unequal on both the outside & inner sides of membranes. The presence (or) absence of these ions is important not only at the triggered state but also at the neuronal resting state. Resting-state:

- Na^+ ion concentration = higher at the outside.
- K^+ ion concentration = higher at the inside.

This iconic separation access right at the membrane, hence creating a chemical gradient across the membrane. Creates an electrical gradient [changes are considered]:

- +ve charge outside
- -ve charge inside

The movement of ions across the membrane needs the help of a protein-embedded channel/ion channel to facilitate their movement. Again, three channels are involved in the transport

- Na^+ channel
- K^+ channel
- Mechanically gated channel

Many channels are open, but some require a signal to open (or) close, i.e., a voltage-gated channel. Some channels are based on change, i.e., ion-gated channels.

5.2 G-PROTEIN-COUPLED RECEPTORS (GPCRs)

G-protein-coupled receptors (GPCRs) are the most frequently targeted receptors for developing novel therapeutics for central nervous system (CNS) disorders.

Integral membrane proteins G-protein-coupled receptors (GPCRs) have an intracellular carboxy terminus, seven transmembrane α-helical domains, and an external amino terminus. A vast array of signals, including photons, ions, proteins, neurotransmitters, and hormones, are recognized by GPCRs.

Cell surface receptors that detect molecules outside the cell and trigger cellular reactions are called G protein-coupled receptors (GPCRs), also referred to as seven-(pass)-transmembrane domain receptors, 7TM receptors, heptahelical receptors, serpentine receptors, and G protein-linked receptors (GPLR). These receptors are a broad class of evolutionarily related proteins. They have G proteins attached to them.

They are sometimes called seven-transmembrane receptors because they pass through the cell membrane seven times in the shape of six loops [2]: three extracellular loops that interact with ligand molecules, three intracellular loops that interact with G proteins, an N-terminal extracellular region, and a C-terminal intracellular region of amino acid residues. Ligands can attach to the binding site inside transmembrane helices (rhodopsin-like family) or the extracellular N-terminus and loops (such as glutamate receptors).

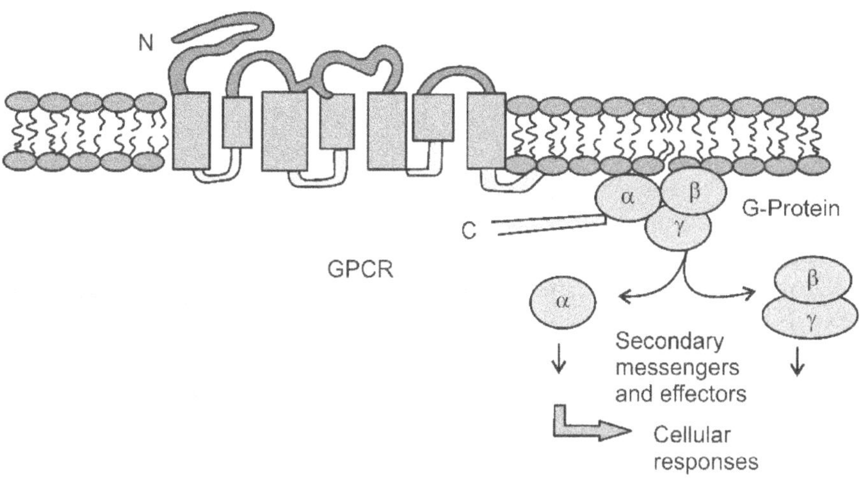

GPCR

With more than 800 members, GPCRs are the biggest family of transmembrane receptors found in humans. Slightly more than half of the 800 receptors are involved in sensory processes that mediate pheromone signaling, taste (33), light perception (10), and smell (400). In the brain, almost 90% (370) of the remaining receptors are expressed. Throughout the human body, these no sensory GPCRs control a number of physiological functions, primarily neurological and endocrine functions, and facilitate signaling from many ligand types. Metabotropic glutamate receptors (especially mGluR5) have been found to be involved in both cognition and Aβ generation and accumulation.

5.3 ENZYMES AS DRUG TARGETS IN CNS

Enzymes: Proteins that act as biological catalysts to accelerate chemical reactions.

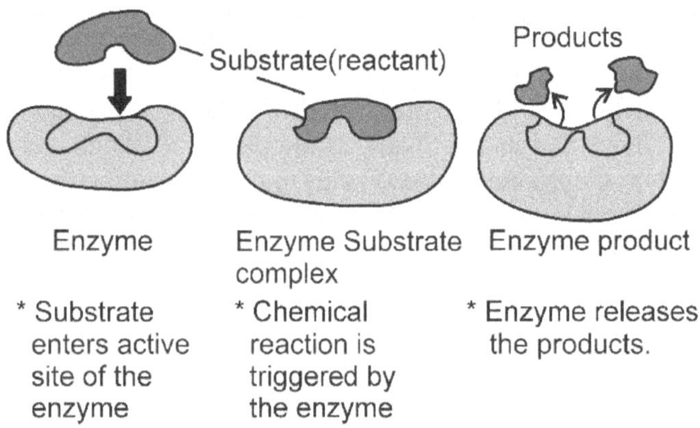

Role of Enzymes in Alzheimer's Disease

β secretase is a key enzyme involved in Aβ production. It cleaves the amyloid precursor protein (APP) to β Amyloid, whose deposition may lead to Alzheimer's disease. β secretase, specifically known as BACE1, is elevated in sporadic Alzheimer's disease, indicating the involvement of this enzyme in the condition.

The elevated enzyme produces Aβ at a higher rate, far exceeding its normal clearance mechanism, resulting in Aβ accumulation and plaque formation. Both the enzymes β and secretase can be targeted to develop novel therapeutic agents to treat Alzheimer's disease.

The Function of Thiamine-Dependent Enzymes in Neurological Conditions. Numerous enzymes depend on the water-soluble vitamin thiamine for proper operation. There is a strong association between its insufficiency and a number of neurological conditions and symptoms. Thiamine pyrophosphokinase in the brain transforms thiamine into thiamine diphosphate (TDP), which is a cofactor for enzymes including transketolase, α ketoglutarate dehydrogenase, and pyruvate dehydrogenase that are involved in glucose metabolism.

A decrease in the activity of α ketoglutarate dehydrogenase results in neuronal cell death, which can lead to pathological manifestations like

Wernicke Korsakoff syndrome characterized by loss of neurons in the thalamus, cerebellum, and midbrain.

Role of DNA Repair Enzymes in Neurological Disorders

Polynucleotide kinase phosphate (PKNP) is an important enzyme that participates in both defective double-strand break repair (DSBR) and single-strand break repair (SSBR). The PKNP makes the ends of the DNA breaks compatible for ligation during DNA repair by using its 3' phosphatase and 5' kinase activity. Neurological problems such as microencephaly with seizures, neurodegeneration, oculomotor apraxia, and dystonia related to impaired DNA repair are caused by a variety of mutations in this enzyme.

Role of Enzymes in Epilepsy

The causes of progressive myoclonic epilepsy include conditions such as GM2 Gangliosidosis, Sandhoff disease, and Tay-Sachs syndrome. Myoclonic epilepsies are also known to be caused by metabolic abnormalities such as hypoglycemia, mitochondrial disorders, and biotin deficiency.GM2 Gangliosidosis is caused by ganglioside accumulation, particularly in the lysosomes. The illness is brought on by abnormalities in the enzymes that catabolize gangliosides.

From an epileptogenic perspective, CDK5 plays a role in maintaining neuronal excitability, synaptic transmission, and synaptic plasticity. CDK5 regulates neurotransmitter release, and its inhibition has led to the release of neurotransmitters and the unmasking of dormant synapses.

Hence, this enzyme is crucial for maintaining the balance between inhibitory and excitatory neurotransmission. Deregulation of CDK5 could lead to an excess neurotransmitter release and hyperexcitability of neurons, leading to epileptogenesis. CDK5 is also thought to cause imbalances in dopamine homeostasis under conditions of elevated glutamate, which leads to excitotoxicity. CDK5 is found to both inhibit and induce epileptogenesis. Under normal physiological conditions, CDK5 inhibits epileptiform activity. But under stressful conditions, due to the high influx of calcium into the cytosol, CDK5 plays the role of inducer of epileptogenesis. This is due to the glutamine-mediated calcium influx via activation of NMDA and AMPA receptors under conditions of stress leading to aberrations in the excitatory feedback circuit. In the case of intractable epilepsy, CDK5 was found to be aberrantly expressed at the transcriptome level. Hence, CDK5 has the potential to be used as a biomarker for epilepsy, especially in drug-resistant cases.

Enzymes in the Pathogenesis of Parkinson's Disease

Reduced dopaminergic signalling is the reason for characteristic symptoms of Parkinsonism, namely, tremors, rigidity, bradykinesia, and postural instability. Enzymes MAO and COMT are involved in the metabolism of dopamine into inactive products. Apart from the administration of L-DOPA, inhibition of these enzymes is an indispensable part of current Parkinson's disease pharmacotherapy. The catecholamine metabolism's free radical byproducts put dopaminergic neurons in the substantia nigra at higher risk of oxidative stress. Neuronal cell loss from unchecked oxidative stress can lead to decreased dopamine signaling and Parkinson's disease. It has been determined that one of the main causes of oxidative stress is the overexpression of the enzyme leucine-rich repeat kinase 2 (LRRK2).

5.4 TRANSPORTERS AND REUPTAKE INHIBITION

TRANSPORTERS

The maintenance of cerebral homeostasis is largely dependent on membrane transport proteins, which are expressed in nearly all cerebral cells and control the flow of various solutes, including endogenous substrates, xenobiotics, and therapeutic drugs. Changes in the expression or activity of CNS transporters have been linked to the development and progression of several neurological disorders. Transporters have recently emerged as promising therapeutic targets to halt or slow the course of neurological diseases.

ABCB1 Transporter

Function: Efflux

Endogenous substrate: Aβ, aldosterone, phospholipids, sphingolipids

Affected diseases: AD, ALS, PD, epilepsy, MS, stroke

ABCG2 Transporter

Function: Efflux

Endogenous substrate: Aβ, bile acid, estrones

Affected diseases: AD, ALS, PD, epilepsy, MS, stroke

CAT-1 Transporter

Function: Uptake

Endogenous substrate: L-arginine, lysine

Affected diseases: AD

LAT1 Transporter

Function: Uptake

Endogenous substrate: tryptophan, methionine, thyroxine

Affected diseases: AD

OATPs Transporter

Function: Uptake

Affected diseases: Stroke

MCTs Transporter

Function: Uptake

Endogenous substrate: Ketone bodies, lactate, pyruvate

Affected diseases: Epilepsy, stroke

REUPTAKE INHIBITION

A reuptake inhibitor's primary goal is to significantly reduce the rate at which neurotransmitters are reabsorbed into the presynaptic neuron, hence raising the synapse's neurotransmitter concentration. As a result, more neurotransmitters attach to pre- and postsynaptic receptors.

Amino acid reuptake inhibition

- Excitatory amino acid reuptake inhibition (or glutamate-aspartate reuptake inhibition)
- GABA reuptake inhibition
- Glycine reuptake inhibition

Monoamine reuptake inhibition

- Dopamine reuptake inhibition
- Norepinephrine reuptake inhibition
- Serotonin reuptake inhibition
- Serotonin-norepinephrine reuptake inhibition
- Norepinephrine-dopamine reuptake inhibition
- Serotonin-dopamine reuptake inhibition
- Serotonin-norepinephrine-dopamine reuptake inhibition.

Miscellaneous

- Adenosine reuptake inhibition
- Endocannabinoid reuptake inhibition.

CHAPTER 6

Antidepressants

Definition

Antidepressants are prescription medications that treat or prevent clinical depression. They can also be used to treat other conditions, like obsessive-compulsive disorder (OCD) and generalized anxiety disorder (GAD)

Classification of Drugs

1. **Tricyclic Antidepressants (TCAs)**
   a. **Serotonin (5-HT) and noradrenaline (NA) reuptake Inhibitors**
      Imipramine, Amitriptyline, Trimipramine
   b. **Predominantly NA reuptake inhibitors**
      Desipramine, Nortriptyline, Amoxapine
2. **Reversible Inhibitors of MAO-A (RIMAs)**
   Moclobemide, Clorgyline
3. **OP Selective Serotonin Reuptake Inhibitors (Ssris)**
   Fluoxetine, Fluvoxamine, Paroxetine, Sertraline, Citalopram, Escitalopram
4. **Serotonin and Noradrenaline Reuptake Inhibitors (Snrls)**
   Venlafaxine, Duloxetine
5. **Atypical Antidepressants**
   Trazodone, Mianserin, Mirtazapine, Bupropion, Tianeptine, Amineptine, Atomoxetine

Mechanism of Action

1. **Selective Serotonin Reuptake Inhibitors (Ssris):** SSRIs work by increasing the levels of serotonin in the brain. Serotonin is a neurotransmitter that plays a key role in regulating mood. SSRIs block the reuptake (reabsorption) of serotonin by certain neurons, which leads to higher serotonin levels in the synapses (gaps between neurons). This increase in serotonin is believed to improve mood and alleviate symptoms of depression and anxiety. **Fluoxetine (20-40mg/day),** a

bicyclic compound, was the pioneering SSRI and boasts the longest duration of action among its class. Its plasma half-life (t½) is 2 days, and its active demethylated metabolite has a t½ of 7–10 days. It has received approval for use in children aged seven and older for treating depression and OCD, with a similar efficacy and side effect profile as seen in adults. Its recommendation for children is contingent on psychotherapy failure. Due to a slower onset of antidepressant effects, it may be less suitable for patients in need of rapid relief but can be a better option for those with poor compliance. **Fluvoxamine (50-200mg/day),** another SSRI, has a shorter duration of action (t½ of 18 hours) and lacks active metabolites. It is specifically recommended for generalized anxiety disorder and OCD rather than depression. Reports indicate relatively more incidents of nausea, dyspepsia, flatulence, nervousness, and discontinuation reactions with fluvoxamine. **Sertraline (50-150mg/day),** a popular SSRI, has gained favour partly due to fewer patients discontinuing treatment due to side effects. It has shown efficacy in juvenile depression and is recommended for anxiety and post-traumatic stress disorder (PTSD). Sertraline is less likely to cause drug interactions due to its impact on CYP isoenzymes. Its plasma t½ is 26 hours, and it generates an even longer-lasting active metabolite. **Citalopram (20-40mg/day),** another SSRI, shares a lower propensity for causing drug interactions with sertraline. Its t½ is 33 hours, and no active metabolite is identified. However, citalopram has recorded a few overdose-related deaths, leading to caution in patients at risk of suicide. It is the preferred SSRI for mood disorders in premenstrual syndrome. **Escitalopram (10-20mg/day),** the active S (+) enantiomer of citalopram, exhibits efficacy at half the dose with similar properties. It presents milder side effects and improved safety.

2. **Serotonin-Norepinephrine Reuptake Inhibitors (SNRIs):** SNRIs, as the name suggests, block the reuptake of both serotonin and norepinephrine. By increasing the levels of these two neurotransmitters in the brain, SNRIs are thought to have a broader effect on mood regulation and are used to treat a range of mood disorders. **Venlafaxine (70-150mg/day)** stands out as a novel antidepressant. Importantly, it does not interact with cholinergic, adrenergic, or histaminergic receptors, nor does it possess sedative properties. Venlafaxine is recognized for its relatively faster onset of action and has demonstrated utility in addressing mood changes, hot flashes in menopausal syndrome, some anxiety disorders, and eating disorders. Common side effects include nausea, sweating, anxiety, dizziness, impotence, and withdrawal reactions upon discontinuation. **Duloxetine (30-80mg/day),** a newer

SNRI like venlafaxine, shares the same non-sedative, non-anticholinergic, and non-antihistaminic characteristics. While it offers milder side effects, including gastrointestinal and sexual problems, some individuals may experience agitation, insomnia, and an increase in blood pressure as potential adverse effects. Duloxetine is also indicated in panic attacks, diabetic neuropathic pain, fibromyalgia, and stress urinary incontinence in women (because it increases urethral tone).

3. **Tricyclic Antidepressants (TCAs):** TCAs inhibit the reuptake of both serotonin and norepinephrine, like SNRIs. Additionally, they block certain receptors, such as histamine and acetylcholine receptors, which can lead to side effects. Reuptake inhibition results in an increased concentration of the amines in the synaptic cleft in both CNS and periphery. Tentative conclusions drawn are:
   - Inhibition of DA uptake correlates with stimulant action but is not primarily involved in antidepressant action.
   - Inhibition of NA and 5-HT uptake is associated with antidepressant action.

   Imipramine (50-200mg/day), an analogue of CPZ, was found during clinical trials (1958) to selectively benefit depressed but not agitated psychotics. These older compounds, in addition to uptake blockade, have direct effects on adrenergic, cholinergic, and histaminergic receptors and are referred to as 'first-generation antidepressants,' a group which also includes MAOIs. The subsequently produced second-generation antidepressants have more selective action on amine uptake.

4. **Monoamine Oxidase Inhibitors (MAOIs):** MAOIs block the enzyme monoamine oxidase, which is responsible for breaking down neurotransmitters like serotonin, norepinephrine, and dopamine. By inhibiting this enzyme, MAOIs increase the levels of these neurotransmitters in the brain. However, MAOIs are less commonly prescribed today due to dietary restrictions and potential drug interactions. The most used is **Moclobemide, 150 mg BD–TDS** (max 600 mg/day) is a reversible and selective inhibitor of MAO-A, and its effects are relatively short-lived; the full activity of MAO is restored within 1–2 days after discontinuation of the medication. Due to its competitive inhibition of the enzyme, tyramine has a limited ability to displace Moclobemide from the enzyme. Consequently, there is minimal enhancement of the pressure response to ingested amines, and dietary restrictions are unnecessary. Nonselective MAO inhibitors produce active metabolites that cause irreversible inactivation of the enzyme. While the drugs themselves have relatively short durations of presence

in the body, their effects persist for 2–3 weeks after discontinuation, earning them the label of 'hit and run' drugs. The restoration of MAO activity hinges on the synthesis of new enzyme molecules, leading to prolonged elevation of tissue monoamine levels even after most of the drug has been eliminated from the body.

5. **Atypical Antidepressants: Trazodone (150mg/day),** as the first atypical antidepressant, exhibits a distinctive profile. It moderately inhibits the uptake of serotonin (5-HT) but also has notable adrenergic effects and acts as a weak antagonist at 5-HT2 receptors. These 5-HT2 antagonistic actions may contribute to its antidepressant effect, albeit with modest efficacy. Trazodone is known for its sedative properties but lacks anticholinergic effects. It tends to lower heart rate (bradycardia) and does not interfere with intracardiac conduction, making it less likely to induce arrhythmias. These characteristics make it a suitable choice for elderly patients. Nausea can be a common side effect, especially at the beginning of treatment. Trazodone has a mild anxiolytic effect and has been found beneficial in some cases of OCD. However, it is worth noting that trazodone has limitations and is infrequently used in depression today. It can cause an uncommon and potentially serious side effect called priapism, which is an inappropriate, prolonged, and painful penile erection. Priapism can lead to impotence in some cases. The α1 adrenergic blocking property of trazodone has been associated with both priapism and postural hypotension. As a result, its use in depression treatment has declined over time.

Pharmacological Actions

1. **Central Nervous System (CNS):** Most antidepressants, including SSRIs, SNRIs, TCAs, and MAOIs, work by increasing the levels of monoamine neurotransmitters such as serotonin, norepinephrine, and, to some extent, dopamine in the synaptic clefts of the brain. This results in improved mood regulation and relief of depressive symptoms.
2. **Autonomic Nervous System:** *Sympathetic and Parasympathetic* **Effects:** TCAs and some atypical antidepressants may block the action of norepinephrine and acetylcholine at peripheral receptors. This can lead to side effects such as dry mouth, constipation, blurred vision, and orthostatic hypotension.
3. **Gastrointestinal System:** *Nausea and GI Disturbances:* Nausea and gastrointestinal upset are common side effects of many antidepressants, particularly SSRIs and SNRIs.

4. **Cardiovascular System:** *QT Interval Prolongation:* Some antidepressants, especially TCAs and certain atypical antidepressants, may cause QT interval prolongation on the electrocardiogram (ECG), which can increase the risk of arrhythmias. TCAs can lower blood pressure upon standing (orthostatic hypotension), leading to dizziness and, in some cases, fainting.
5. **Endocrine System:** Antidepressants can influence the hypothalamic-pituitary-adrenal (HPA) axis, which plays a role in the body's stress response and hormone regulation. Chronic stress and depression can affect the HPA axis, and antidepressants may help normalize its function.
6. **Immune System:** Some studies suggest that certain antidepressants may have anti-inflammatory effects by modulating cytokine levels. Chronic inflammation is thought to be associated with depression, and these drugs may help reduce inflammation.
7. **Reproductive System:** *Sexual Dysfunction:* Many antidepressants, especially SSRIs and SNRIs, can cause sexual side effects, including decreased libido, erectile dysfunction, and delayed ejaculation.
8. **Metabolic System:** *Weight Gain:* Some antidepressants, such as mirtazapine and certain SSRIs, are associated with weight gain, which may be due to changes in appetite and metabolism.

Pharmacokinetics

Most antidepressants are administered orally, typically in the form of tablets or capsules. The drug is absorbed through the gastrointestinal tract, and the rate of absorption varies depending on the specific drug. Some should be taken with food to reduce gastrointestinal side effects, while others should be taken on an empty stomach for optimal absorption. Many antidepressants bind to plasma proteins, primarily albumin. This binding affects the drug's distribution within the bloodstream and its availability for action at target sites. The ability of different antidepressants to penetrate the blood-brain barrier varies. Antidepressants undergo extensive hepatic metabolism in the liver by enzymes of the cytochrome P450 (CYP) system. Dosing adjustments may be necessary for individuals with impaired kidney function. Some antidepressants are excreted via the bile into the gastrointestinal tract and then eliminated in faces.

Half-Life: The half-life of antidepressants varies widely. Selective Serotonin Reuptake Inhibitors (SSRIs) have a half-life ranging from about 20 to 35 hours, and Serotonin-Norepinephrine Reuptake Inhibitors (SNRIs) often around 5 to 15 hours. While TCAs like amitriptyline and imipramine tend to have longer half-lives, often ranging from 10 to 80 hours, and MAOIs typically have longer half-lives, often exceeding 24 hours.

Adverse Drug Reactions

1. **Common Adverse Reactions:**
   a. **Nausea and Gastrointestinal Upset:** Many antidepressants, particularly SSRIs and SNRIs, can cause nausea, vomiting, diarrhea, or other gastrointestinal discomfort. Taking these medications with food or adjusting the timing of doses may help alleviate these symptoms.
   b. **Sleep Disturbances:** Antidepressants can affect sleep patterns. Some individuals may experience insomnia or vivid dreams, while others may feel excessively drowsy.
   c. **Sexual Dysfunction:** Sexual side effects are common with many antidepressants, including decreased libido, difficulty achieving or maintaining an erection (erectile dysfunction), and delayed ejaculation.
   d. **Weight Changes:** Weight gain or weight loss can occur with certain antidepressants. TCAs, mirtazapine, and some SSRIs are more likely to be associated with weight gain.
2. **Less Common Adverse Reactions**
   a. **Dizziness and Orthostatic Hypotension:** Some antidepressants, particularly TCAs, can cause low blood pressure, leading to dizziness and a drop in blood pressure when changing positions (orthostatic hypotension).
   b. **Sedation:** Certain antidepressants, like mirtazapine and trazodone, can have sedating effects, leading to daytime drowsiness.
   c. **Anxiety or Agitation:** Paradoxically, some individuals may experience increased anxiety, restlessness, or agitation when taking antidepressants, especially in the initial weeks of treatment.
   d. **Serotonin Syndrome:** This is a rare but potentially life-threatening condition that can occur when there is an excessive accumulation of serotonin in the body. It can result from combining certain antidepressants or taking them with other medications that affect serotonin.
   e. **Allergic Reactions:** Although uncommon, some individuals may develop allergic reactions to antidepressant medications, which can manifest as skin rashes, itching, swelling, or difficulty breathing.

3. **Rare but Serious Adverse Reactions**
   a. **Suicidal Thoughts:** In some cases, particularly among children, adolescents, and young adults, antidepressant use may be associated with an increased risk of suicidal thoughts or behavior. This risk is closely monitored, especially when initiating treatment.
   b. **Serious Cardiac Effects:** Certain antidepressants, such as TCAs, may have potential cardiac side effects, including arrhythmias and QT interval prolongation. This can be life-threatening in some cases.
   c. **Hepatotoxicity:** Rarely, certain antidepressants may cause liver damage, leading to elevated liver enzymes and jaundice.
   d. **Blood Disorders:** TCAs have been associated with rare blood disorders such as agranulocytosis and thrombocytopenia.
4. **Withdrawal Symptoms:** Discontinuing antidepressants abruptly or too rapidly can lead to withdrawal symptoms. These can include flu-like symptoms, dizziness, irritability, mood swings, and electric shock sensations (brain zaps). It is important to taper off these medications under medical supervision.

Contraindications

1. Hypersensitivity or Allergy
2. MAOIs have significant dietary restrictions due to the risk of a hypertensive crisis when certain foods high in tyramine are consumed (e.g., aged cheeses, cured meats, and certain alcoholic beverages).
3. Concurrent Use of MAOIs and Other Antidepressants
4. Combining MAOIs with other antidepressants, including SSRIs, SNRIs, and TCAs, can lead to a potentially life-threatening condition known as serotonin syndrome.
5. Seizures
6. Some antidepressants, particularly bupropion (Wellbutrin), have a lower seizure threshold. They should be used with caution or avoided in individuals with a history of seizures or conditions that increase seizure risk.
7. TCAs should be used cautiously or avoided in individuals who have recently experienced a myocardial infarction due to their potential to cause cardiac arrhythmias.
8. Pregnancy and Breastfeeding
9. Age and Paediatric Populations

Therapeutic Uses

1. **Major Depressive Disorder (MDD):** Antidepressants can alleviate the core symptoms of depression, including low mood, loss of energy, changes in appetite, sleep disturbances, and thoughts of self-harm or suicide.
2. **Generalized Anxiety Disorder (GAD):** Certain antidepressants, especially SSRIs and SNRIs, are effective in reducing the symptoms of GAD. They help decrease excessive anxiety, nervousness, and physical symptoms like muscle tension and restlessness.
3. **Panic Disorder:** SSRIs are used to reduce the frequency and severity of panic attacks. They help individuals regain control over their anxiety and panic symptoms.
4. **Social Anxiety Disorder (Social Phobia):** SSRIs and SNRIs can help reduce the symptoms of social anxiety. They can ease the fear of social interactions and improve the ability to engage in daily activities.
5. **Obsessive-Compulsive Disorder (OCD):** Certain antidepressants, especially SSRIs, are considered first-line treatments for OCD. They can help reduce the frequency and intensity of obsessions and compulsions.
6. **Post-Traumatic Stress Disorder (PTSD):** SNRIs are often used as part of the treatment plan for PTSD. They can help alleviate the intrusive symptoms and improve overall functioning.

6.1 ANTI-MANIC DRUGS

Definition

Antimanic drugs, also known as mood stabilizers, are medications used to treat and manage manic episodes in individuals with bipolar disorder. Manic episodes are characterized by symptoms such as elevated mood, excessive energy, impulsivity, and sometimes psychosis.

Classification

1. **Lithium**

   Lithium Carbonate: Lithium is the classic and most well-known mood stabilizer. It is an element, not a compound, and its exact mechanism of action is not fully understood. It is believed to modulate neurotransmitter activity, particularly in the brain's circuitry involved in mood regulation.

2. **Anticonvulsant Mood Stabilizers**

   a) Valproate (Valproic Acid): Valproate is an anticonvulsant that is also effective as a mood stabilizer. It is thought to increase the availability of the inhibitory neurotransmitter GABA (gamma-aminobutyric acid).

   b) Lamotrigine: Lamotrigine is another anticonvulsant used as a mood stabilizer. It may reduce the release of excitatory neurotransmitters like glutamate.

   c) Carbamazepine: Carbamazepine is an anticonvulsant that affects sodium channels in nerve cells, helping to control mood swings.

   d) Atypical Antipsychotics: Risperidone

Mechanism of Action

1. **Lithium:** Lithium is among the most utilized mood stabilizers for individuals with bipolar disorder. Although the precise mechanism remains somewhat unclear, there are several proposed ways in which lithium exerts its effects:

- Lithium partially replaces sodium ions (Na+) in the body and is distributed relatively evenly both inside and outside cells, which may influence the flow of ions across brain cells or modify the properties of cell membranes. However, it's important to note that the therapeutic concentration of lithium is much lower compared to sodium and potassium ions.
- Lithium reduces the release of norepinephrine (NA) and dopamine (DA) in the brain, specifically in animal studies, without impacting the release of serotonin (5-HT). This action may help correct any imbalances in the turnover of brain monoamines.
- A compelling hypothesis suggests that lithium's therapeutic effects are related to its inhibition of inositol-1-phosphate hydrolysis by inositol monophosphatase. This inhibition results in a reduction in available free inositol, which is essential for regenerating membrane phosphatidylinositides. These phosphatidylinositides serve as the source of inositol trisphosphate (IP3) and diacylglycerol (DAG), both of which are important for signal transduction within cells. This mechanism is believed to selectively affect hyperactive neurons associated with manic states, as the supply of inositol from external sources is limited. Consequently, lithium may target overactive

receptors, indirectly dampening signal transduction through the phosphatidylinositol pathway.

- **Adverse effects** include nausea, vomiting, and mild diarrhoea, which occur initially and can be minimized by starting at lower doses. Thirst and polyuria are experienced by most; some fluid retention may occur initially but clears later. Fine tremors are noted even at therapeutic concentrations. CNS toxicity manifests as plasma concentration rises, producing coarse tremors, giddiness, ataxia, motor incoordination, nystagmus, mental confusion, slurred speech, and hyper-reflexia. Overdose symptoms are regularly seen at plasma concentrations above two mEq/L. In acute intoxication, these symptoms progress to muscle twitching, drowsiness, delirium, coma, and convulsions. Vomiting, severe diarrhoea, albuminuria, hypotension, and cardiac arrhythmias are the other features.
- **Drug Interactions** Diuretics (thiazide, furosemide), by causing Na^+ loss promote proximal tubular reabsorption of Na^+ as well as Li^+ → plasma levels of lithium rise. Potassium-sparing diuretics cause milder Li^+ retention. Tetracyclines, NSAIDs, and ACE inhibitors can also cause lithium retention. Lithium reduces the pressor response to NA. Lithium tends to enhance insulin/sulfonylurea-induced hypoglycaemia. Succinylcholine and pancuronium have produced prolonged paralysis in lithium-treated patients. Neuroleptics, including haloperidol, have been frequently used along with lithium without problem. However, sometimes, the combination of haloperidol and lithium produces marked tremor and rigidity. The neuroleptic action appears to be potentiated by lithium.

2. **Anticonvulsants (e.g., Valproic Acid, Lamotrigine, Carbamazepine):** Anticonvulsant mood stabilizers work by regulating the activity of neurotransmitters and ion channels in the brain. **Valproic acid** is believed to increase the availability of gamma-aminobutyric acid (GABA), a neurotransmitter that has inhibitory effects on brain activity. This helps calm overexcited brain regions associated with mania. **Lamotrigine** may help stabilize mood by reducing the release of excitatory neurotransmitters like glutamate. **Carbamazepine** affects sodium channels in nerve cells, which can help control mood swings. Atypical antipsychotic drugs can be used as mood stabilizers in bipolar disorder. They primarily work by blocking the action of dopamine, a neurotransmitter associated with pleasure and reward. This can help reduce the

intensity of manic symptoms. Some atypical antipsychotics also affect serotonin receptors, which can influence mood regulation.

3. **Antidepressants (used with caution):** In some cases, antidepressant medications may be prescribed alongside mood stabilizers to manage depressive symptoms in bipolar disorder. Antidepressants often work by increasing the levels of neurotransmitters like serotonin and norepinephrine in the brain. However, their use in bipolar disorder can be controversial, as they may trigger manic episodes in some individuals.

Pharmacokinetics

The absorption of anti-manic drugs can differ widely among various medications. Some mood stabilizers, such as lithium, are readily absorbed from the gastrointestinal tract after oral administration. Lithium carbonate and lithium citrate are common oral forms. Anticonvulsant mood stabilizers like valproate and lamotrigine are also well-absorbed orally. Atypical antipsychotic mood stabilizers are available in oral forms and are absorbed from the gastrointestinal tract. After absorption, these drugs are distributed throughout the body via the bloodstream. Mood stabilizers may cross the blood-brain barrier to reach their target sites in the brain, where they exert their effects on mood regulation. The distribution of these drugs can vary, with some having a relatively wide distribution in the body and others having more specific tissue targeting. The metabolism of anti-manic drugs occurs primarily in the liver through various enzymatic processes. Individual drugs have distinct metabolic pathways. For example, valproate is metabolized in the liver, primarily by the enzyme glucuronyl transferase.

Some drugs, like lithium, have limited metabolism and are excreted largely unchanged in the urine. The elimination of these drugs is primarily through the renal system (kidneys) in the form of metabolites or unchanged drugs. For example, lithium has a relatively long half-life, which can be influenced by factors such as renal function and hydration status. Regular monitoring of blood levels is often necessary to maintain therapeutic drug concentrations within the desired range.

Pharmacological Actions

Lithium can help reduce the intensity of manic episodes and stabilize mood by affecting neurotransmitter activity and possibly influencing the flow of ions across nerve cell membranes. **Anticonvulsant Mood Stabilizers** may increase the availability of inhibitory neurotransmitters like GABA (gamma-aminobutyric acid) or regulate neurotransmitter release, which helps control mood swings. **Atypical Antipsychotic Mood Stabilizers** help control manic symptoms by influencing the activity of neurotransmitters associated with mood regulation. **Valproate**, an anticonvulsant mood stabilizer, may affect other mechanisms, such as inhibiting inositol-1-phosphate hydrolysis by inositol mono phosphatase. This action reduces the availability of free inositol, impacting signal transduction pathways involved in mood regulation.

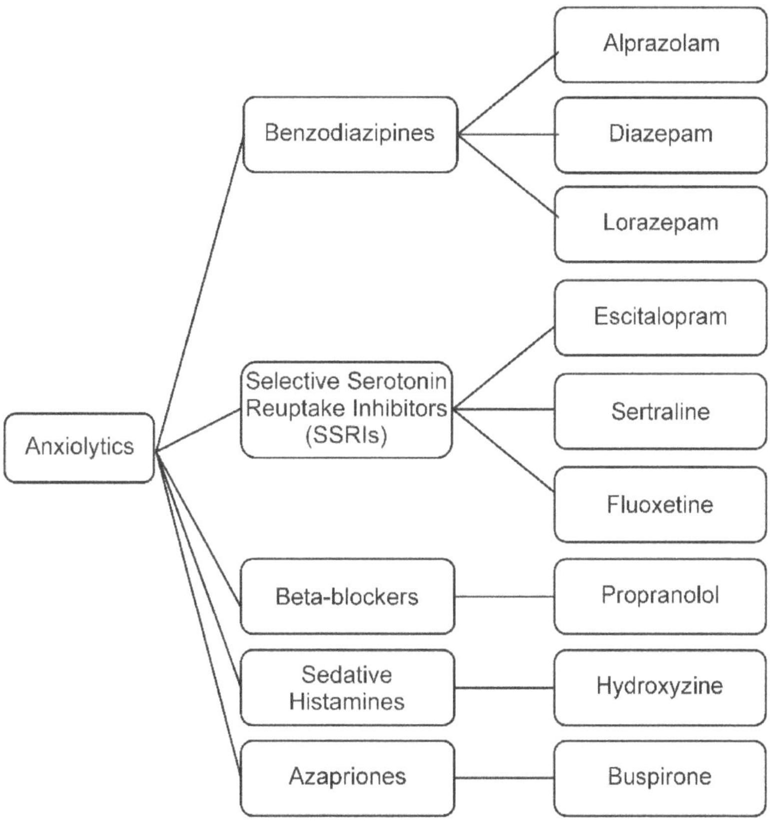

6.2 ANXIOLYTIC AND HYPNOTIC DRUGS

Definition

Anxiolytics are drugs used to treat anxiety and are called anti-anxiety drugs. Anti-anxiety drugs are used to treat Anxiety disorders, Panic disorders, Generalized anxiety, Depression, and Insomnia.

Classification of Drugs

1. **Benzodiazepines**

   Examples: Diazepam, Alprazolam, Lorazepam, Clonazepam.

   Mechanism of Action: Benzodiazepines work by enhancing the inhibitory effects of the neurotransmitter gamma-aminobutyric acid (GABA) in the central nervous system. They bind to specific receptors known as GABA-A receptors. GABA is an inhibitory neurotransmitter that reduces the activity of neurons. When benzodiazepines bind to GABA-A receptors, they increase the frequency of chloride channel opening in response to GABA, leading to increased chloride ion influx into neurons. This hyperpolarizes the neuron, making it less likely to fire and transmit signals, which results in a calming and anxiolytic effect.

   Pharmacokinetics

   Well-absorbed orally, with a rapid onset and high lipid solubility, they distribute widely throughout the body. Metabolized in the liver into active metabolites and excreted in urine.

   Therapeutics: Benzodiazepines are used for the short-term treatment of severe anxiety, panic disorders, and acute stress reactions and as adjuncts in the management of alcohol withdrawal.

   ADRs: Common side effects include drowsiness, dizziness, memory impairment, and risk of dependence. They can also cause paradoxical reactions (increased anxiety or agitation).

   Drug Interactions: Benzodiazepines can interact with other central nervous system depressants, including alcohol and opioids, leading to enhanced sedation and respiratory depression.

   Contraindications: Contraindicated in individuals with a history of substance abuse, pregnancy (especially in the first trimester), and those with severe liver disease.

2. **Selective Serotonin Reuptake Inhibitors (SSRIs)**

   Examples: Escitalopram, Sertraline, Fluoxetine.

   Mechanism of Action: SSRIs block the reuptake of serotonin in the synaptic cleft, which is the gap between two neurons. Serotonin is a neurotransmitter involved in mood regulation. When SSRIs inhibit the reuptake of serotonin, more serotonin remains in the synaptic cleft, allowing it to continue binding to serotonin receptors on the receiving neuron. This leads to increased serotonin signaling and, over time, can help regulate mood and reduce anxiety.

Pharmacokinetics: Generally well-absorbed orally, metabolized in the liver, and excreted in urine.

Therapeutics: Used to treat generalized anxiety disorder, panic disorder, and social anxiety disorder, as they have a lower risk of dependence compared to benzodiazepines.

ADRs: Common side effects include nausea, sexual dysfunction, and the potential for serotonin syndrome in overdose. Discontinuation syndrome can occur when stopping SSRIs abruptly.

Drug Interactions: SSRIs can interact with other drugs that affect serotonin levels, potentially leading to serotonin syndrome.

Contraindications: Contraindicated in individuals taking monoamine oxidase inhibitors (MAOIs) due to the risk of serotonin syndrome.

3. **Buspirone: Mechanism of Action:** Buspirone's mechanism of action is different from that of benzodiazepines and SSRIs. It acts as a partial agonist of serotonin (5-HT1A) receptors and as an antagonist of dopamine (D2) receptors. By partially activating serotonin receptors and blocking dopamine receptors, buspirone modulates neurotransmitter activity. This modulation results in anxiolytic effects without causing sedation or dependence. The precise way buspirone works to reduce anxiety is not fully understood, but it is believed to involve changes in neurotransmitter balance.

   Pharmacokinetics: Well-absorbed orally, metabolized in the liver, and excreted in urine.

   Therapeutics: Used for the treatment of generalized anxiety disorder.

   ADRs: Generally well-tolerated, but side effects can include dizziness, headache, and nausea. It has a delayed onset of action and is not suitable for acute anxiety.

   Drug Interactions: Buspirone may interact with drugs that inhibit the metabolism of CYP3A4 enzymes.

   Contraindications: Contraindicated in individuals with a history of hypersensitivity to buspirone.

4. **Beta-Blockers**

   Examples: Propranolol, Atenolol.

   Mechanism of Action: Beta-blockers like propranolol work by blocking beta-adrenergic receptors in the body. These receptors are typically activated by adrenaline (epinephrine) and norepinephrine, which are released during the "fight or flight" response. By blocking these receptors, beta-blockers reduce the physiological symptoms of anxiety, such as increased heart rate, tremors, and sweating. This action helps prevent the physical manifestations of anxiety, particularly in situations like public speaking or performance anxiety.

Pharmacokinetics: Variable depending on the specific beta-blocker used.

Therapeutics: Primarily used to manage performance anxiety (e.g., stage fright).

ADRs: Side effects may include fatigue, bradycardia, and hypotension.

Drug Interactions: Beta-blockers can interact with other drugs that affect blood pressure and heart rate.

Contraindications: Contraindicated in individuals with certain heart conditions and asthma.

6.3 ANTIPSYCHOTICS

Definition

Antipsychotic medications, also known as neuroleptics, are a class of drugs used to manage various mental health conditions, primarily psychotic disorders. These drugs are used to alleviate symptoms of psychosis, such as hallucinations, delusions, thought disturbances, and disorganized thinking.

Antipsychotics are also used to treat Schizophrenia.

Classification

1. **Phenothiazines**
    - **Aliphatic side chain:** Chlorpromazine, Triflupromazine
    - **Piperidine side chain:** Thioridazine
    - **Piperazine side chain:** Trifluoperazine, Fluphenazine
2. **Atypical antipsychotics**
    - Clozapine
    - Aripiprazole
    - Risperidone
    - Ziprasidone
3. **Butyrophenones Haloperidol**
    - Trifluperidol
    - Penfluridol

4. **Thioxanthenes**
    - Flupenthixol
5. **Other heterocyclics**
    - Pimozide,
    - Loxapine

Mechanism of Action

- The major and common pharmacological effect of all antipsychotic medication is they modulate the positive symptoms of Schizophrenia.
- Recall that these are the symptoms associated with psychosis—hallucinations, delusions, and thought disorders.
- This antipsychotic effect is achieved by blocking D2 receptors and reducing dopamine transmission in the limbic system, consistent with the dopamine hypothesis of Schizophrenia.
- Atypical antipsychotics, such as clozapine, can reduce positive symptoms of Schizophrenia and have a greater effect on negative symptoms (e.g., flat affect, alogia, and lack of interest or pleasure).
- This is due to the dual mechanism of action of atypical neuroleptics.
- Like typical neuroleptics, these second-generation drugs retain the ability to block D2 receptors to reduce positive signs.
- Initially, they were considered atypical because they produced minimal extrapyramidal motor disturbance.
- Subsequently, it was noted that these neuroleptics were more effective than first-generation drugs in reducing negative signs of Schizophrenia, which are largely mediated by serotonin receptors in the limbic system.

The figure below shows the neurochemical effects of atypical antipsychotics on dopamine and serotonin transmission. Positive symptoms of Schizophrenia are associated with the overactivation of D2 receptors, while negative symptoms are associated with the overactivation of 5-HT2A receptors. Atypical neuroleptics are antagonists at both receptors, which provides them with a broader spectrum of antipsychotic activity than typical neuroleptic drugs.

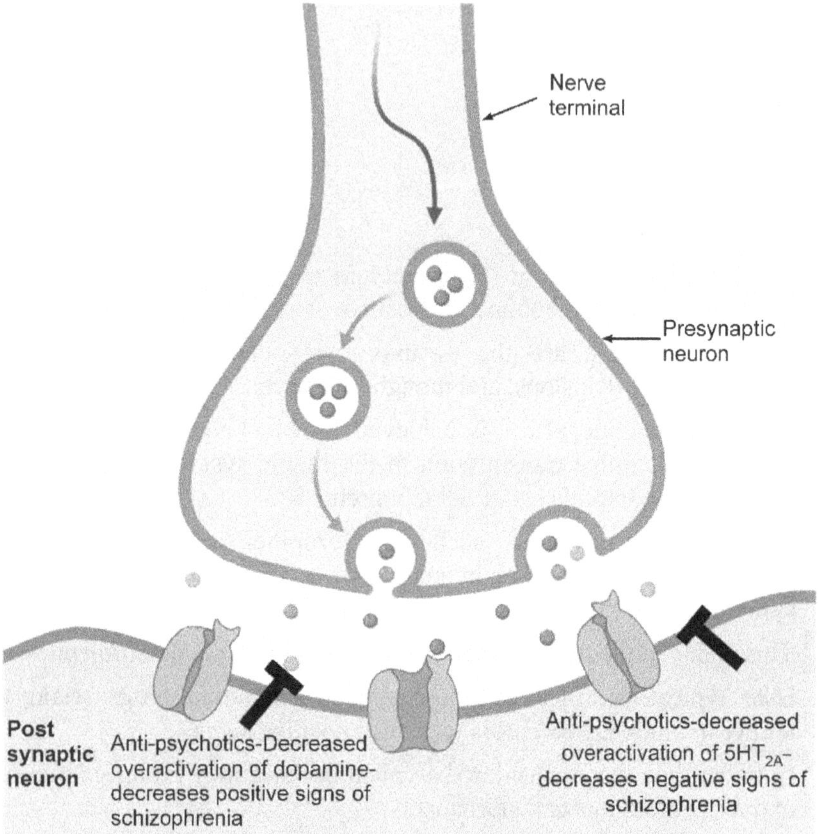

Fig.6.1 Mechanism of action of Ant-psychotics or neuroleptics.

Pharmacological Actions

1. **CNS** Effects differ in normal and psychotic individuals.
   - **Among individuals without mental illness**, CPZ induces a state of indifference towards their surroundings, a decrease in thought richness, slower physical movements, emotional dampening, diminished drive, and a tendency to fall asleep easily, yet they can be readily awakened.
   - While spontaneous movements are decreased, issues like slurred speech, ataxia, or motor coordination problems do not typically arise.
   - This collection of symptoms is termed the 'neuroleptic syndrome' and differs notably from the sedative effects seen with barbiturates and similar substances.
   - **In individuals with psychosis**, CPZ mitigates irrational behaviors, restlessness, and aggression, effectively managing psychotic

symptoms. Over time, disordered thoughts and behaviors tend to normalize while anxiety is alleviated. Hyperactivity, hallucinations, and delusions are suppressed.

- The sedative properties of CPZ manifest swiftly, while its antipsychotic effects may take weeks to manifest fully. Additionally, tolerance tends to develop towards its sedative effects but not towards its antipsychotic effects, suggesting these two effects operate independently.

2. **ANS**
   - Neuroleptics exhibit varying degrees of increased adrenergic blocking activity, with the hierarchy being: CPZ = triflupromazine = thioridazine > clozapine > fluphenazine > haloperidol > trifluoperazine > pimozide. In other words, more potent compounds generally display lower levels of adrenergic-blocking activity. The anticholinergic property of neuroleptics is relatively weak and can be ranked as follows: thioridazine > CPZ > triflupromazine > trifluoperazine = haloperidol. Additionally, phenothiazines possess weak H1-antihistaminic and anti-5-HT actions.

3. **CVS**
   - Neuroleptics induce hypotension, particularly postural hypotension, through both central and peripheral actions on sympathetic tone. However, hypotension is not a prominent feature in psychotic patients but can be exacerbated by hypovolemia. At high doses, CPZ directly depresses the heart and can lead to electrocardiogram (ECG) changes such as Q-T prolongation and suppression of the T wave. CPZ also exhibits some antiarrhythmic effects, likely attributable to membrane stabilization. However, arrhythmias may occur in cases of overdose, particularly with thioridazine.

4. **Skeletal Muscle**
   - Neuroleptics do not directly impact muscle fibres or neuromuscular transmission. Nevertheless, they do diminish specific types of spasticity, with their action site believed to be in the basal ganglia or medulla oblongata. Importantly, spinal reflexes remain unaffected by their administration.

5. **Endocrine**
   - Neuroleptics continuously boost the release of prolactin by inhibiting dopamine's suppressive effect on pituitary lactotropes. This can lead to the development of galactorrhea and gynecomastia.

Pharmacokinetics

- **Oral absorption** of CPZ is somewhat unpredictable, and bioavailability is low. More consistent effects are produced after i.m. or i.v. Administration.
- It is **highly bound to plasma** as well as tissue proteins; brain concentration is higher than plasma concentration.
- **The volume of distribution**, therefore, is large (20 L/kg). It is metabolized in the liver, mainly by CYP 2D6, into several metabolites.
- The acute effects of a single dose of CPZ generally last for **6–8 hours**.
- The **elimination** t½ is variable but mostly is in the range of 18– 30 hours.
- Nevertheless, **therapeutic effects** may be seen at 30–200 ng/ml.
- The **metabolites are excreted** in urine and bile for months after discontinuing the drug.

Adverse Drug Reaction

CNS Effects: Drowsiness, lethargy, mental confusion. Tolerance to sedative effects may develop.

Cardiovascular (CVS) Effects: Postural Hypotension, Palpitation, Q-T prolongation, cardiac arrhythmias (thioridazine, pimozide, ziprasidone).

Anticholinergic Effects: Dry mouth, blurred vision, constipation, urinary hesitancy (notable with thioridazine).

Endocrine Effects: Hyperprolactinemia, amenorrhoea, infertility, galactorrhoea, gynaecomastia.

Metabolic Effects: Diabetes Risk

Drug Interactions

1. Neuroleptics potentiate all CNS depressants hypnotics, anxiolytics, alcohol, opioids, and antihistaminics.
2. Neuroleptics blocks- levodopa and direct DA agonists in parkinsonism.

Indications or Uses

- **Psychoses-** *Schizophrenia, Mania, Organic brain Syndromes,*
- **Anxiety**
- **Anit-emetics**

Psychomimetics

(Hallucinogens, Psychedelics, Psychodysleptics, Psychotogens)

These are substances that change mood, behavior, thinking, and perception in a way reminiscent of psychosis.

- **Psychotomimetics:** drugs that are used to mimic psychosis
- **Psychedelics:** Drugs that help in mind-expanding
- **Psychodysleptics:** any agent that has alterations in perception, cognition, and mood as its primary psychobiological actions in the presence of a clear sensorium
- **Psychotogens:** a substance that causes a psychotic reaction.

- Hallucinogens are a class of psychoactive drugs that can alter states of consciousness, causing changes to perception, mood, and thought.

1. **Indole Amines**
   - **Lysergic acid diethylamide (LSD):** It was discovered by Hofmann in 1938 during his research on ergot alkaloids. It's the most potent psychedelic, with effects noticeable at doses as low as 25–50 µg. Apart from its psychological effects, it also stimulates the central nervous system. Its mechanism of action involves serotonin neuronal systems in the brain.
   - **Lysergic acid amide:** Like LSD but less potent; found in morning glory seeds.
   - **Psilocybin:** Derived from the Mexican mushroom Psilocybe mexicana, traditionally used by indigenous tribes in religious ceremonies.
   - **Harmine:** Present in the Banisteriopsis caapi vine from the Amazon region, historically used by Brazilian natives as a snuff.
   - **Bufotenin:** Isolated from the skin of the toad Bufo marinus, also found in 'Cohaba Snuff' and the mushroom Amanita muscaria. These compounds are all Indolealkylamines, chemically related to serotonin (5-HT). Various synthetic derivatives like Dimethyltryptamine (DMT) also exhibit hallucinogenic properties.

2. **Phenylalkyl Amines**
   - **Mescaline:** Derived from the Mexican 'Peyote cactus' Lophophora Williams, used in native rituals, though it is relatively low in potency.

3. Arylcyclohexyl Amines

- **Phencyclidine (PCP):** An anticholinergic compound that induces disorientation, body image distortion, hallucinations, and anesthetic-like effects by activating σ receptors in the brain. Ketamine, a related compound, is used in anesthesia but also abused recreationally.

Hallucinogens, notably marijuana, induce dream-like states with altered perception, loss of reality contact, and vivid hallucinations. While they can induce relaxation and euphoria, higher doses may lead to panic reactions. Tolerance may develop, but physical dependence is rare. Despite their potential therapeutic uses, hallucinogens are primarily considered drugs of abuse.

6.4 ADDICTION (ALCOHOL AND METHYL ALCOHOL) AND DISULFIRAM

Ethanol is eliminated from the body via zero-order kinetics. In chronic alcoholics, the enzyme CYP2E1, which metabolizes paracetamol, is induced, leading to an increased production of its toxic metabolite.

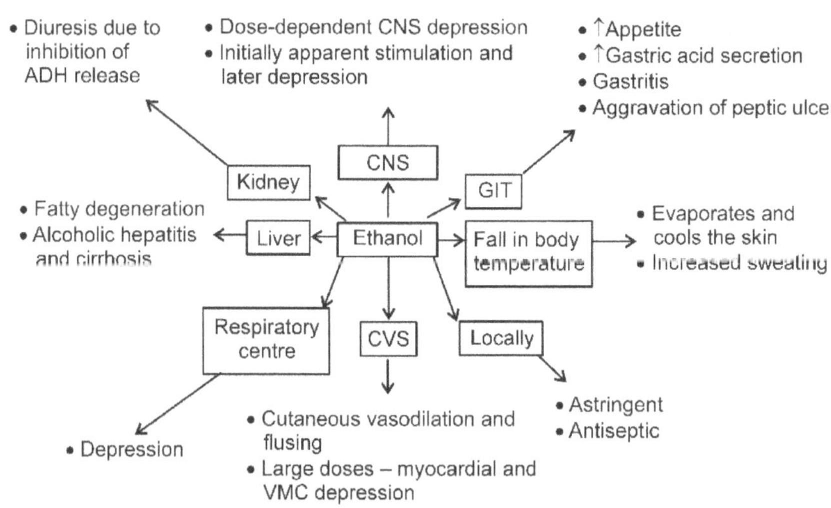

Therapeutic Uses of Ethanol

1. Antiseptic

- 70% ethanol is commonly used as a skin antiseptic before injections or surgeries.
- Higher concentrations (>90%) reduce antiseptic efficacy.

- It should not be applied to open wounds, mucosa, ulcers, or the scrotum due to its irritant nature.
- Not suitable for disinfecting instruments, as it causes rusting.

2. **Neuralgia Relief**
   - Alcohol injections into nerve trunks provide pain relief by destroying the nerves.
3. **Prevention of Bedsores**
   - Local application of alcohol prevents bedsores in immobile patients.
4. **Methanol Poisoning**
   - Ethanol competes with methanol for metabolic enzymes, preventing the formation of toxic metabolites like formaldehyde and formic acid.
5. **Fever Management**
   - Alcoholic sponges help lower body temperature in febrile conditions.

Acute Ethanol Overdose (Alcohol Intoxication)

Symptoms
Drowsiness, nausea, vomiting, ataxia, hypotension, respiratory depression, and hypoglycemia.

Treatment

- This is a medical emergency. The focus is on preventing severe respiratory depression and aspiration of vomit.
- Ensure proper airway, breathing, and circulation (ABC).
- Manage fluid and electrolyte balance. Gastric lavage may be required.
- Intravenous glucose corrects hypoglycemia, and thiamine is given via infusion.
- Hemodialysis accelerates recovery in severe cases.

Alcohol Withdrawal Syndrome

Cause
Abrupt cessation or reduction of alcohol in chronic users.

Symptoms
Restlessness, tremors, insomnia, nausea, vomiting, hallucinations, delirium, convulsions, and possible collapse.

Treatment

- Benzodiazepines (BZDs): Drugs like diazepam and chlordiazepoxide manage anxiety, tremors, palpitations, sleep disturbances, confusion, and seizures.
- Psychological support is critical.

Treatment of Alcohol Withdrawal Syndrome

BZDs (diazepam, chlordiazepoxide, etc.) are used to control anxiety, tremor, palpitations, sleep disturbances, confusion, and convulsions associated with alcohol withdrawal and psychological support.

Treatment of Chronic Alcoholism

(a) Disulfiram (alcohol aversion therapy): It causes aversion to alcohol.

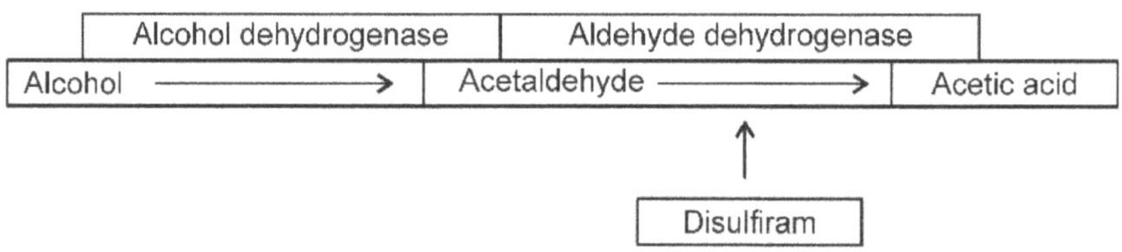

Disulfiram inhibits aldehyde dehydrogenase and causes the accumulation of acetaldehyde in blood and tissues (acetaldehyde syndrome). The signs and symptoms include nausea, vomiting, flushing, headache, sweating, tachycardia, palpitation, breathlessness, chest pain, hypotension, hypoglycaemia, confusion, shock, and even death. This reaction is unpleasant; hence, a person on disulfiram develops an aversion to alcohol.

Drugs like metronidazole, griseofulvin, and cefoperazone also have disulfiram-like action and produce similar reactions with alcohol. Doctors should warn patients not to take alcohol and alcohol-containing products when they are on the above-mentioned drugs.

(b) Naltrexone (opioid antagonist): It reduces alcohol craving and helps to maintain abstinence.

Methanol Poisoning

Cause

Occurs from consuming methylated spirits or alcohol adulterated with methanol.

Pathophysiology

Methanol is metabolized into formaldehyde and formic acid, leading to metabolic acidosis and retinal damage.

Symptoms

Nausea, vomiting, abdominal pain, headache, vertigo, confusion, hypotension, convulsions, coma, metabolic acidosis, vision dimness, and blindness.

Treatment

- **Eye Protection:** Keep the patient in a dark room to prevent retinal damage.
- **Supportive Care:** Maintain airway, breathing, and circulation.
- **Gastric Lavage:** Perform after endotracheal intubation.
- **Sodium Bicarbonate:** Administer intravenously to correct acidosis and prevent retinal damage.
- **Ethanol Administration**
    - Ethanol (10%) is given via nasogastric tube.
    - Ethanol competes with methanol for metabolic enzymes, reducing the formation of toxic metabolites.
    - Methanol is excreted unchanged in urine and breath.

CHAPTER 7

Drugs used in Pain Management

7.1 SEDATIVES, HYPNOTICS, AND CENTRAL ACTING MUSCLE RELAXANTS

Definition

Sedatives are medications that calm individuals without necessarily inducing sleep, although they may cause drowsiness. Sedation results in reduced responsiveness to stimulation, accompanied by decreased motor activity and cognitive processes.

Hypnotics, on the other hand, are drugs that either induce or sustain sleep resembling normal, easily arousable sleep. This differs from the concept of hypnosis, which involves a trance-like state characterized by passivity and high susceptibility to suggestions.

Both sedatives and hypnotics act as central nervous system depressants, but they vary in their onset, duration, and dose-response patterns. Hypnotics typically have a quicker onset, shorter duration, and steeper dose-response curve, making them preferable for inducing sleep. Conversely, sedatives tend to act more slowly with flatter dose-response curves. However, there is an overlap between the two categories, as a hypnotic at a lower dose may function as a sedative. Thus, the spectrum of CNS depression ranges from sedation to hypnosis to general anesthesia.

At high doses, hypnotics can induce general anesthesia. However, benzodiazepines (BZDs) differ from other CNS depressants like barbiturates in that they are not considered nonselective or global depressants. The primary application of sedatives and hypnotics is in treating insomnia.

Classification

1. **Barbiturates**

   Long-acting Short-acting Ultra-short acting

   Phenobarbitone Butobarbitone Thiopentone

   Pentobarbitone Methohexitone

2. **Benzodiazepines**

Hypnotic Antianxiety Anticonvulsant

Diazepam Diazepam Diazepam

Flurazepam Chlordiazepoxide Lorazepam

Nitrazepam Oxazepam Clonazepam

Alprazolam Lorazepam Clobazam

Temazepam Alprazolam

Triazolam

3. **Newer nonbenzodiazepine hypnotics**

Zopiclone Zolpidem Zaleplon

BARBITURATES

Barbiturates have been popular hypnotics and sedatives of the last century up to the 1960s, but are not used now to promote sleep or to calm patients. However, they are described first because they are the prototype of CNS depressants. Barbiturates are substituted derivatives of barbituric acid (malonyl urea). Barbituric acid, as such, is not a hypnotic but compounds with alkyl or aryl substitution on C5 are. Replacement of O with S at C2 yields thiobarbiturates which are more lipid-soluble and more potent. Barbiturates have variable lipid solubility; the more soluble ones are more potent and shorter-acting. They are insoluble in water, but their sodium salts dissolve, yielding a highly alkaline solution.

PHARMACOLOGICAL ACTIONS

Barbiturates are general depressants for all excitable cells, and the CNS is the most sensitive, where the effect is almost global, but certain areas are more susceptible.

1. CNS Barbiturates produce dose-dependent effects:

sedation → sleep → anaesthesia → coma.

Benzodiazepines

All BZDs have a benzene ring fused to a seven-membered diazepine ring.

Sites of action: Midbrain (ascending reticular formation), limbic system, brain stem, etc.

Mechanism of Action

BZDs facilitate the action of GABA - they potentiate the inhibitory effects of GABA.

But BZDs have no GABA-mimetic action

Benzodiazepines

↓

Bind to specific site on GABAA receptor (different from GABA-binding site)

↓

Increase in frequency of opening Cl channels

↓

Increase in GABA-mediated chloride current

↓

Membrane hyperpolarization

↓

CNS depression

Pharmacological Actions and Therapeutic Uses

1. **Sedation and Hypnosis:** BZDs decrease the time required to fall asleep (sleep latency). The total sleep time is increased. They shorten all stages of NREM sleep except stage 2, which is prolonged. The duration of REM sleep is usually decreased. BZDs reduce night awakenings and produce refreshing sleep. At present, BZDs are preferred to barbiturates for the treatment of short-term insomnia because they have a wide therapeutic index and cause near-normal sleep and fewer rebound phenomena on withdrawal. They produce minimal hangover effects (headache and residual drowsiness on waking). They cause minimal respiratory depression.
2. **Anticonvulsant:** Diazepam, lorazepam, clonazepam, clobazam, etc. have anticonvulsant effect. Intravenous (i.v.) diazepam/lorazepam is used to control life-threatening seizures in status epilepticus, tetanus, drug-induced convulsions, febrile convulsions, etc. Clonazepam is used in the treatment of absence seizures.
3. **Diagnostic (Endoscopies) and Minor Operative Procedures:** i.v. BZDs are used because of their sedative-amnesic-analgesic and muscle relaxant properties.

4. **Preanaesthetic Medication and General Anaesthesia (Ga):** These drugs are used as pre-anesthetic medication because of their sedative-amnesic and anxiolytic effects. Hence, the patient cannot recall the perioperative events later. i.v. diazepam, lorazepam, midazolam, etc. are combined with other CNS depressants to produce GA.
5. **Anxiety (Anxiolytic) Effect:** Some BZDs (diazepam, oxazepam, alprazolam, lorazepam, chlordiazepoxide, etc.) have selective antianxiety action at low doses. The anxiolytic effect is due to their action on the limbic system. Tolerance to the antianxiety action of BZDs develops only on prolonged use.
6. **Muscle Relaxant (Centrally Acting):** They reduce skeletal muscle tone by inhibiting polysynaptic reflexes in the spinal cord. The relaxant effect of BZDs is useful in spinal injuries, tetanus, and cerebral palsy and to reduce spasms due to joint injury or sprain.

Pharmacokinetics

BZDs are usually given orally or intravenously and occasionally by rectal route (diazepam) in children. The rate of absorption following oral administration is variable. They have a large volume of distribution. They have a short duration of action on occasional use because of rapid redistribution; hence, they are free of residual (hangover) effects, even though the elimination half-life is long. BZDs are metabolized in the liver. The metabolites are excreted in urine. BZDs cross the placental barrier.

Adverse Effects

BZDs have a wide margin of safety. They are generally well tolerated. The common side effects are drowsiness, confusion, blurred vision, amnesia, disorientation, tolerance, and drug dependence. Withdrawal after chronic use causes symptoms like tremors, insomnia, restlessness, nervousness, and loss of appetite. Use of BZDs during labour may cause respiratory depression and hypotonia in newborns (Floppy baby syndrome). In some patients, these drugs may produce paradoxical effects, i.e., convulsions and anxiety.

Barbiturates

All barbiturates are derivatives of barbituric acid. They are nonselective CNS depressants and act at many sites, the ascending reticular activating system (ARAS) being the main site.

Mechanism of Action

Barbiturates have GABA facilitatory action; they potentiate the inhibitory effects of GABA.

Barbiturates
↓
Bind to GABAA receptor (different from BZD-binding site)
↓
The duration of Cl channel kept open is increased
↓
Increase in GABA-mediated chloride current
↓
Membrane hyperpolarization
↓
CNS depression

Pharmacological Actions and Uses

1. **Sedation and Hypnosis**

   Barbiturates were historically used for treating insomnia due to their ability to reduce sleep latency and suppress REM sleep, as well as stages 3 and 4 of NREM sleep. However, they significantly disrupt normal sleep patterns and are no longer recommended because of the drawbacks such as low therapeutic index, rebound REM sleep increase upon discontinuation, severe respiratory depression, pronounced hangover effects, such as headache and next-day drowsiness, high potential for tolerance and dependence.

2. Ultrashort-acting barbiturates like thiopentone and methohexitone are used for the induction of general anesthesia.

3. Phenobarbitone is effective in managing status epilepticus and generalized tonic-clonic seizures (GTCS).

4. In cases of non-hemolytic neonatal jaundice, phenobarbitone may lower serum bilirubin levels by inducing glucuronyl transferase, an enzyme that aids in bilirubin metabolism.

Adverse Effects

Common side effects include drowsiness, confusion, headache, ataxia, hypotension, and respiratory depression. Hypersensitivity reactions, such as skin rashes, facial swelling, and itching, may occur, and prolonged use leads to tolerance for sedative and hypnotic effects. Extended phenobarbitone use may result in megaloblastic anemia due to impaired folic acid absorption.

Management of Acute Barbiturate Poisoning

- Ensure airway, breathing, and circulation are maintained.
- Correct electrolyte imbalances.
- Perform gastric lavage followed by activated charcoal to enhance drug elimination. For unconscious patients, intubation is done before lavage to protect the airway.
- Administer intravenous sodium bicarbonate to alkalinize the urine, promoting barbiturate excretion since they are weak acids.
- In severe cases, hemodialysis may be required.

Drug Interactions

Barbiturates induce hepatic microsomal enzymes, which can decrease the efficacy of co-administered medications such as oral contraceptives, anticoagulants, and hypoglycemic agents.

Non-Benzodiazepine Hypnotics

Drugs like zolpidem, zopiclone, zaleplon, eszopiclone, and etizolam have lower abuse potential compared to benzodiazepines (BZDs). They exhibit weaker anxiolytic, anticonvulsant, and muscle relaxant properties and minimally affect REM sleep.

Zolpidem

- Primarily used for short-term treatment of insomnia, zolpidem reduces sleep latency and increases total sleep duration with minimal alteration in REM sleep.
- It produces near-normal sleep patterns, with reduced hangover effects and a lower risk of tolerance or dependence.
- Administered orally, zolpidem is rapidly absorbed, metabolized in the liver, and excreted through urine.
- Flumazenil can reverse its effects.
- Common side effects include headache, confusion, nausea, and vomiting.

Mechanism of Action

Zolpidem, zopiclone, zaleplon, eszopiclone
(nonbenzodiazepine hypnotics)

↓

Bind selectively to BZD binding site on GABAA receptor

↓

Facilitate GABA-mediated neuronal inhibition

↓

CNS depression

7.2 GENERAL ANAESTHETICS

General Anaesthetics refer to drug-induced reversible loss of consciousness and all sensations. **The features of GA** are as follows:

1. Reversible loss of consciousness.
2. Reversible loss of sensation.
3. Analgesia and amnesia.
4. Muscle relaxation and abolition of reflexes.

Mechanism of Action of General Anaesthetics

The main site of action of anaesthetics is reticular formation, which normally maintains a state of consciousness. Most anaesthetics decrease transmission in reticular formation by enhancing the activity of inhibitory transmitters like GABA (e.g., BZDs, barbiturates, and propofol) and blocking the activity of excitatory transmitters (e.g., blockade of N-methyl-D-aspartate [NMDA] glutamate receptors by ketamine and nitrous oxide).

Stages of General Anaesthesia

STAGE I: It is the state of analgesia because the sensory transmission in the spinothalamic tract is inhibited. There is no amnesia. Consciousness and sense of touch are present, while sense of hearing is enhanced.

STAGE II: It is the state of excitement and delirium. The patient shows violent behaviour and is amnesic. There is an irregular rise in blood pressure and respiratory rate. To avoid these symptoms, a short-acting barbiturate like thiopental sodium is given intravenously before administration of inhalation anaesthetic.

STAGE III: It is the stage of surgical anaesthesia. Regular respiration and relaxation of skeletal muscle occur during this stage. It is divided into the following four planes:

Plane 1: During this plane, there are revolving movements of eyeballs which, while attaining plane 3, get fixed. Respiration and skeletal muscle tone are normal.

Plane 2: Most surgical procedures are performed during this plane. There is a progressive loss of corneal, light, and laryngeal reflexes. Respiration is slow but regular.

Plane 3: It is a plane of marked muscle relaxation. Respiration is abdominal. Eyeball movement is absent. Pupils are dilated. Light, corneal, and laryngeal reflexes are absent.

Plane 4: It is a plane of complete muscle relaxation. Pupils are dilated. There is a complete loss of light, as well as corneal and laryngeal reflexes. Respiration is abdominal.

STAGE IV: It is a stage of medullary paralysis. It appears to be due to an overdose of the general anaesthetic. During this stage, there is severe depression in the respiratory centre and vasomotor centre in the medulla. The stage is fatal, causing the death of the patient.

The most reliable index for attainment of stage III is loss of corneal reflex and establishment of regular respiratory pattern. A fall in BP cardiac and respiratory depression are the signs of deep anaesthesia. As against this, resistance to insertion.

Pharmacokinetic Principles

There are three factors that need attention. They are induction, maintenance, and recovery. The principles of pharmacokinetics should be understood in the context of these factors.

Induction

It means the time interval between the administration of an anaesthetic drug and the development of the stage of surgical anaesthesia. Lipophilicity is the key factor governing the pharmacokinetics of inducing drugs. Being highly lipophilic, after a single intravenous bolus injection, these drugs preferentially enter the brain. Redistribution out of CNS into muscle, viscera, and lipophilic adipose tissue are the main causes for termination of action.

Maintenance

It is the period during which the patient remains in a sustained stage of surgical anaesthesia (stage III, plane-2). During this stage, the anaesthesiologist monitors the patient's vital signs and response to various stimuli by controlling the concentration of anaesthetic to be inhaled or infused based on the depth of the anaesthesia. The factors which influence the uptake and distribution of the anaesthetic govern the rate at which an effective concentration of the anaesthetic reaches the brain. This requires the transfer of anaesthetic from the alveolar air to the blood and then to the brain. The rate of transfer depends on the following factors:

- Alveolar wash-in
- Solubility characteristic of anaesthetic drug
- The concentration of the drug in the inspired air
- The pulmonary ventilation rates
- Cardiac output
- The partial pressure gradient of the drug between arterial and venous blood before its redistribution

Recovery

The recovery phase starts when the anaesthetic drug is discontinued. During this phase, the anaesthesiologist has to ensure that there are no delayed toxic reactions. Frequently, oxygen is given during the last few minutes of anaesthesia and in the early post-anaesthetic period. Metabolism of anaesthetic is an important factor during recovery. The gradation of metabolism of anaesthetics by the liver is as follows: methoxyflurane > halothane > enflurane > sevoflurane > isoflurane > desflurane > nitrous oxide. Nitrous oxide is almost totally washed out by exhalation.

Classification

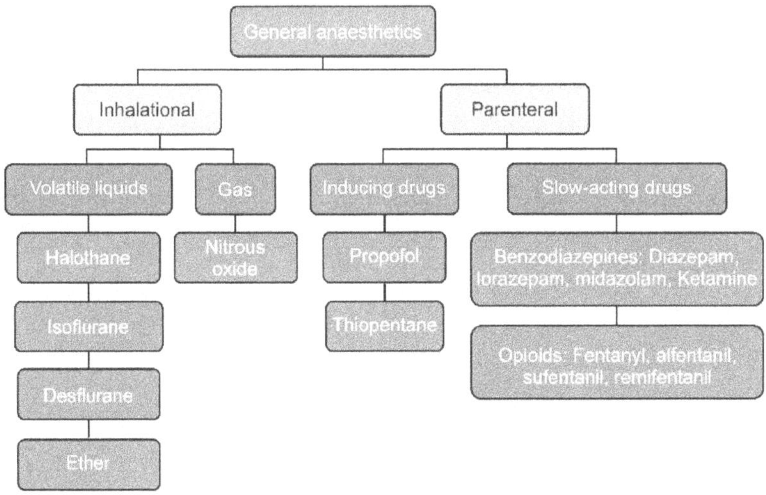

Inhalational Anaesthetics

Mechanism of Action of Inhalation Anesthetics

- Inhalation anesthetics act by interacting with hydrophobic regions of neuronal membrane proteins, disrupting their function.
- GABA-mediated effects: Drugs like barbiturates, benzodiazepines, etomidate, and propofol enhance GABA action, increasing chloride ion flux and inhibiting neuronal activity.
- NMDA receptor blockade: Ketamine blocks glutamate action at NMDA receptors, reducing excitatory neurotransmission.
- Cholinergic synapses: Anesthetics like enflurane and isoflurane reduce the excitatory effects of acetylcholine by shortening the opening of nicotine receptor sodium channels.
- Overall, anesthetics disrupt neuronal firing, particularly in the thalamus and cerebral cortex, leading to loss of consciousness, analgesia, and reduced motor activity.

The potency of Inhalation Anesthetics

- **Potency is measured using Minimum Alveolar Concentration (MAC)**
  - The concentration required to prevent movement in 50% of patients in response to a surgical incision.
  - Smaller MAC values indicate greater potency.
  - Higher lipid solubility corresponds to lower MAC values.

- **Factors Affecting MAC**
  - o Decreases with age, hypothermia, and CNS depressants like sedatives and opioids.
  - o Not affected by sex, species, acid-base balance, or blood pressure.
- **MAC Values (Descending Potency)**
- Methoxyflurane (0.16%) > Halothane (0.75%) > Isoflurane (1.2%) > Enflurane (1.7%) > Sevoflurane (1.9%) > Desflurane (6%) > Nitrous oxide (> 100%).
- *Nitrous Oxide:* Least potent, as even 100% inhalation does not achieve 1 MAC.

Specific Inhalation Anesthetics

1. Nitrous Oxide

- Mild, sweet-smelling, non-inflammable gas.
- Used with 30% oxygen and other agents like halothane or propofol for surgical anesthesia.
- **Effects**
  - o Strong analgesic (50% nitrous oxide + 50% oxygen = effects similar to morphine).
  - o Rapid induction and recovery (4 minutes).
  - o No significant effects on the cardiovascular, respiratory, renal, or hepatic systems.
- **Limitations**
  - ▪ Low potency.
  - ▪ No bronchodilation or muscle relaxation.
  - ▪ Prolonged use (>4 hours) can cause bone marrow changes (megaloblastic anemia).

2. Halothane

- Halogenated volatile anesthetic with a mild, sweet odor.
- Non-irritant, non-inflammable, and relatively inexpensive.
- **Effects**
  - o Poor analgesic and muscle relaxants; often combined with nitrous oxide, opioids, or muscle relaxants.
  - o Suitable for general anesthesia but requires supplementation for pain and muscle relaxation.

Parenteral General Anesthetics

1. Inducing Drugs

1. Propofol

- **Formulation:** Available as a 1% emulsion for intravenous (i.v.) administration, propofol is a widely used anesthetic with rapid onset and short duration of action.
- **Mechanism of Action:** Acts on GABA receptors to enhance chloride ion conductance, leading to neuronal hyperpolarization and central nervous system (CNS) depression.
- **Pharmacokinetics:** Rapidly metabolized in the liver and excreted in urine. It is highly plasma protein-bound and crosses the placental barrier, making it suitable for use in pregnant women.
- **Uses and Benefits**

1. Rapid induction and recovery with minimal residual symptoms.
2. Ideal for outpatient surgical procedures.
3. Non-irritant to airways, making it safe for asthmatics.
4. Has antiemetic properties, reducing postoperative nausea and vomiting.
5. Suitable for both induction and maintenance of anesthesia via continuous infusion or repeated doses.

2. Thiopentone Sodium: An ultra-short-acting barbiturate commonly used for induction of anesthesia has high lipid solubility, allowing rapid penetration into highly perfused organs like the brain, liver, and heart. Redistribution to less perfused tissues, such as skeletal muscle and adipose tissue, terminates its action. It can be administered as a 2.5% solution.

Uses

1. Induction of anesthesia.
2. Occasional use as an anticonvulsant.
3. Subanesthetic doses are used for narcoanalysis in psychiatry.

Adverse Effects: Respiratory and cardiovascular depression, risk of laryngospasm, and contraindicated in acute intermittent porphyria due to induction of ALA synthase.

3. Ketamine produces "dissociative anesthesia," characterized by sedation, amnesia, profound analgesia, and dissociation from surroundings, which can block NMDA glutamate receptors.

Ketamine is highly lipid-soluble; it quickly enters highly perfused organs and is metabolized in the liver, with excretion via urine and bile. It causes sympathetic stimulation, increasing heart rate, blood pressure, and cardiac output, and is often used in hypovolemic patients and is well-tolerated by children. Ketamine is majorly used for procedures involving the head, neck, and face and is ideal for dressing burn wounds.

Adverse Effects and Contraindications

1. Increases blood pressure and intracranial pressure, contraindicating its use in hypertensive or ischemic heart disease patients.
2. May cause the emergence of delirium and hallucinations.

7.3 LOCAL ANESTHETICS

Local Anesthetics (LAs)

Local anesthetics are drugs that, when applied topically or injected locally, block nerve conduction and cause a temporary loss of sensation in the area supplied by the affected nerve. The order of nerve function blockade is as follows: pain → temperature → touch → pressure → skeletal muscle power.

Classification of Local Anesthetics

1. Based on Clinical Use

- **Surface Anesthetics:** Cocaine, lignocaine, tetracaine, benzocaine, oxethazaine, proparacaine, butylaminobenzoate.
- **Injectable Anesthetics:**
  - **Short-acting, low potency:** Procaine, chloroprocaine.
  - **Intermediate-acting, moderate potency:** Lignocaine, mepivacaine, prilocaine, articaine.
  - **Long-acting, high potency:** Tetracaine, bupivacaine, dibucaine, ropivacaine.

2. Based on Chemical Structure

- **Esters:** Cocaine, procaine, chloroprocaine, benzocaine, tetracaine.
- **Amides:** Lignocaine, mepivacaine, bupivacaine, prilocaine, articaine, ropivacaine.

Mechanism of Action

Local anesthetics **act on voltage-gated sodium (Na^+) channels**. Sodium channels cycle through three states: resting, open, and inactivated. For an impulse to occur, the channel must transition from the inactivated state to the resting state.

Local anesthetics in their **unionized form** penetrate the nerve sheath and axon membrane. Once inside the axoplasm, they become **ionized** and block voltage-gated Na^+ channels, preventing the conduction of nerve impulses and thereby inducing a localized, reversible loss of sensation.

Local anaesthetics are weak bases

At tissue pH (7.4)

Partly unionized   Partly ionized

↓

Penetrate the nerve membrane

↓

Enter the axon (axonal pH is low)

↓

Reionization of local anaesthetics

↓

LA gains access to its receptor in the open state of the channel

↓

Las block the voltage-gated Na+ channel from inside; binds more tightly to inactivated state, prolongs the inactivated state

↓

Prevent entry of Na+ ions into the neuron - **decreasing the rate of depolarization**

↓

Prevent generation of action potential

↓

No generation and conduction of impluses to CNS

↓

Local anaesthesia

Factors Affecting Local Anesthetic (LA) Action

- **pKa (Acid Dissociation Constant):** Drugs with a higher pKa have a greater ionized fraction at physiological pH, leading to a slower onset of action. For example, procaine (pKa 9.1) has a slow onset, while lignocaine (pKa 7.7) has a rapid onset. However, despite chloroprocaine's high pKa (9.1), it exhibits a rapid onset of action due to other contributing factors.

- **Plasma Protein Binding:** Drugs with higher plasma protein binding have a prolonged duration of action. For instance, procaine has minimal plasma protein binding and a short duration of action, whereas bupivacaine, which is highly bound to plasma proteins, has a longer duration.

2. **Diffusion Rate from the Site of Administration:** The onset of action depends on the initial concentration gradient. A higher drug concentration at the site results in faster diffusion and quicker onset.
3. **Lipid Solubility:** Greater lipid solubility increases the potency of the anesthetic. For example, lignocaine is more potent than procaine due to its higher lipid solubility.
4. **Presence of Vasoconstrictors** like adrenaline prolongs the duration of action by reducing systemic absorption of the anesthetic, thus retaining it at the administration site.

Pharmacological Actions

1. **Nervous System**

   Peripheral Nerves: Autonomic fibers are blocked first, followed by somatic fibers. The blockade order is: pain → temperature → touch → pressure → motor functions.

   Central Nervous System (CNS)

   Most LAs cross the blood-brain barrier. Initially, they cause CNS stimulation (excitement, tremors, twitching, convulsions), followed by depression at higher doses, which can lead to respiratory failure, coma, and death.

2. **Cardiovascular System (CVS)**

   Heart: LAs block sodium channels, reducing abnormal pacemaker activity, contractility, conductivity, and cardiac output. They increase the effective refractory period. At high concentrations, LAs can precipitate cardiac arrhythmias. Lignocaine decreases automaticity and is used for treating ventricular arrhythmias.

   Blood Vessels: LAs cause vasodilation and myocardial depression, leading to hypotension.

Pharmacokinetics

- **Metabolism:** Ester-linked LAs are rapidly metabolized by plasma cholinesterase, and Amide-linked LAs are primarily metabolized in the liver.
- **Oral Effectiveness:** LAs like procaine and lignocaine are ineffective orally due to significant first-pass metabolism.
- **Considerations in Liver Disease:** Amide-linked LAs such as lignocaine require dose adjustments in patients with liver dysfunction due to impaired metabolism.

Adverse Effects

1. **CNS:** Initial stimulation (restlessness, tremor, headache, confusion) followed by depression (respiratory failure, coma, and death).
2. **CVS:** Bradycardia, hypotension, cardiac arrhythmias, and, in severe cases, cardiovascular collapse. Bupivacaine is highly cardiotoxic.
3. **Allergic Reactions:** Ester-linked LAs have a higher risk of allergic reactions compared to amide-linked LAs. Symptoms include skin rashes, itching, urticaria, bronchospasm, and rare anaphylaxis.
4. **Other Reactions:**
   - Cocaine can cause mucosal irritation.
   - Prilocaine may induce methemoglobinemia.
   - Methylparaben, a preservative in some LA formulations, may trigger allergic reactions.

Techniques of Local Anesthesia

1. **Surface (Topical) Anesthesia**
   - Applied to broken skin or mucous membranes (e.g., nose, mouth, eyes, throat).
   - **Common uses:** diagnostic procedures like eye tonometry or endoscopies and for minor injuries or burns.
   - **Examples:** Tetracaine (2%), lignocaine (2–10%), benzocaine (1–2%), available as creams, sprays, gels, etc.

Key Points

- The motor function remains unaffected.

- Adrenaline doesn't prolong its effect because of poor penetration.
- EMLA is used for intact skin and superficial tissues.

2. **Infiltration Anesthesia**
    - LA is injected into tissues around the surgical site, blocking sensory nerves.
    - **Common drugs:** Lignocaine (0.5–1%), procaine (0.5–1%), bupivacaine (0.125–0.25%).
    - **Adding adrenaline (1:50,000–250,000) prolongs its effect.**
    - **Uses:** Suitable for small procedures like abscess drainage, suturing, or minor surgeries.

Limitations

- Requires large amounts of drug for small areas.
- Avoid if there is an infection or clotting disorder.

Conduction Block Techniques

1. **Field Block Anesthesia**
    - LA is injected under the skin to numb an area distal to the injection site.
    - Used for minor procedures on the scalp, abdominal wall, or limbs.
    - Advantages: A small dose covers a large area.
2. **Nerve Block Anesthesia**
    - LA is injected near a specific nerve or nerve plexus to block sensation in a larger area.

Examples

- Brachial plexus block: Upper limb surgeries.
- Cervical plexus block: Neck surgeries.
- Intercostal nerve block: Abdominal wall surgeries.
- Sciatic/femoral nerve block: Surgeries below the knee.

Advantages: Requires Less LA than Field or Infiltration Methods.

Spinal Anesthesia

- **Procedure:** LA is injected into the subarachnoid space to numb spinal nerve roots.
- **Injection Site:** Between L2-L3 or L3-L4, below the spinal cord.

- **Factors Influencing Effectiveness:**
  - Injection site and volume.
  - Injection force and drug density (hyperbaric, hypobaric, or isobaric).
  - Patient's position (prone, lateral, or tilted).
- **Common Drugs Used:** Lignocaine, tetracaine, bupivacaine (adrenaline can prolong effects).
- **Uses**
  - Surgeries below the umbilicus, such as lower limb procedures, C-sections, prostatectomy, appendectomy, and perineal surgeries.

CHAPTER 8

Neurological Disorders

8.1 NEURODEGENERATIVE DISEASES (PARKINSONISM AND ALZHEIMER'S DISEASE)

Drugs Used in Parkinsonism

Definition

Parkinsonism is a motor disorder marked by rigidity, tremors, and slow movement, with secondary effects like poor posture, mask-like face, and excessive salivation. Untreated, it worsens over the years, leading to immobility and respiratory failure.

Dopamine Pathways Affected by Parkinson's Disease

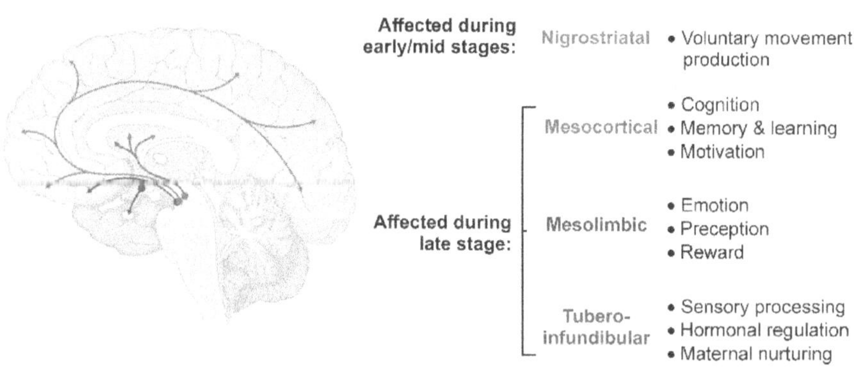

Classification of Drugs for Parkinsonism

I. **Drugs affecting the brain dopaminergic system**

   (a) **Dopamine precursor:** Levodopa (l-dopa)

   (b) **Peripheral decarboxylase inhibitors:** Carbidopa, Benserazide

   (c) **Dopaminergic agonists:** Bromocriptine, Ropinirole, Pramipexole

(d) **MAO-B inhibitors:** Selegiline, Rasagiline

(e) **COMT inhibitors:** Entacapone, Tolcapone

(f) **Glutamate (NMDA receptor) antagonist (Dopamine facilitator):** Amantadine

II. Drugs Affecting the Brain Cholinergic System

(a) **Central anticholinergics:** Trihexyphenidyl (Benzhexol), Procyclidine, Biperiden

(b) **Antihistaminics:** Orphenadrine, Promethazine

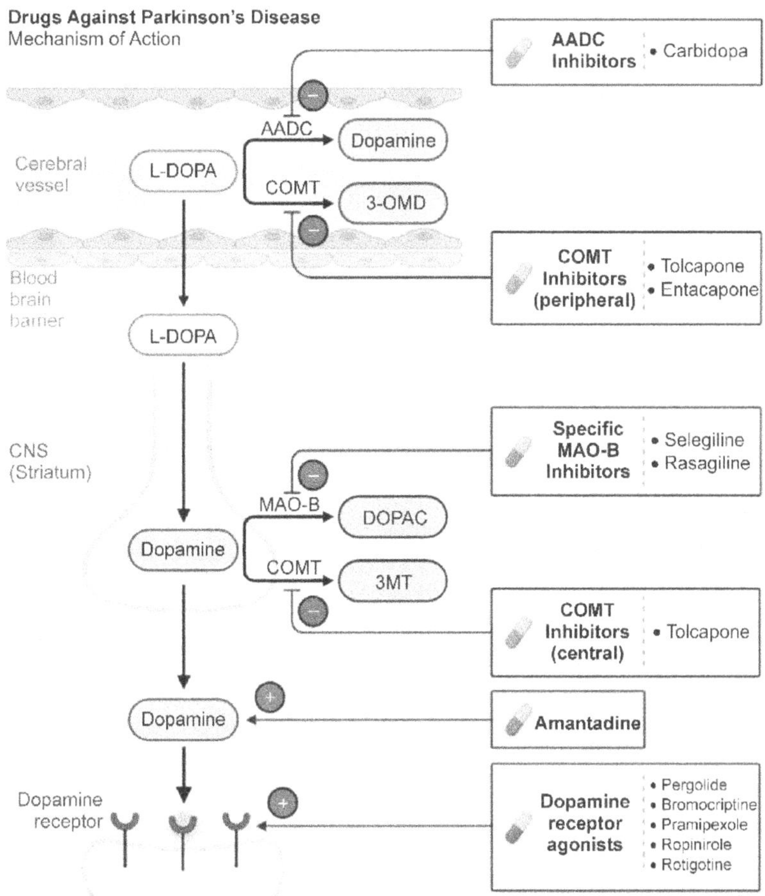

Levodopa and Carbidopa

Levodopa is highly effective in treating Parkinson's disease (PD), more so than any other drug used alone. It is the direct precursor to dopamine (DA), but over 95% of an oral dose is broken down in peripheral tissues like the gut and liver. The remaining DA affects the heart, blood vessels, and the chemoreceptor trigger zone (CTZ) in the brain, which isn't protected by the blood-brain barrier. Only 1–2% of levodopa reaches the brain, which is converted into DA by surviving neurons. Studies show patients treated with levodopa have higher brain DA levels, and those who responded well had even higher levels than those who didn't respond as well.

Mechanism of Action

a) **Levodopa:** Because Parkinsonism results from insufficient dopamine in specific regions of the brain, attempts have been made to replenish the dopamine deficiency. Dopamine itself does not cross the blood-brain barrier, but its immediate precursor, levodopa, is actively transported into the CNS and is converted to dopamine in the brain (see Figure 8.6). Large doses of levodopa are required because much of the drug is decarboxylated to dopamine in the periphery, resulting in side effects that include nausea, vomiting, cardiac arrhythmias, and hypotension.

b) **Carbidopa:** Carbidopa, a dopa decarboxylase inhibitor, diminishes the metabolism of levodopa in the gastrointestinal tract and peripheral tissues, thereby increasing the availability of levodopa to the CNS. Adding carbidopa lowers the dose of levodopa needed by four- to fivefold and, consequently, decreases the severity of the side effects arising from peripherally formed dopamine.

Actions

Levodopa helps reduce rigidity, tremors, and other symptoms of Parkinsonism.

Therapeutic Uses

Levodopa combined with carbidopa is a highly effective treatment for Parkinson's disease. It significantly alleviates symptoms in about two-thirds of patients, especially during the first few years of treatment. However, the effectiveness usually decreases after 3 to 5 years of use.

Absorption and Metabolism

Levodopa is quickly absorbed from the small intestine when the stomach is empty. It has a short half-life of 1 to 2 hours, leading to fluctuations in plasma levels that can cause varying motor responses, such as the "on-off" phenomenon, where motor control changes unpredictably. High-protein meals interfere with levodopa absorption because amino acids (like leucine and isoleucine) compete with it for absorption and transport into the brain. Therefore, levodopa should be taken on an empty stomach, ideally 45 minutes before meals. Any withdrawal from the drug should be done gradually.

Adverse Effects

Peripheral Effects: Common side effects include anorexia, nausea, and vomiting, which are due to stimulation of the chemoreceptor trigger zone in the medulla. Cardiac effects can include tachycardia and ventricular extrasystoles from dopaminergic activity on the heart, as well as hypotension. Adrenergic effects can lead to mydriasis (dilation of the pupils). In some cases, patients may experience blood dyscrasias and a positive Coombs test reaction. Additionally, saliva and urine may appear brownish due to melanin produced from catecholamine oxidation.

CNS Effects: Levodopa can lead to visual and auditory hallucinations, as well as abnormal involuntary movements known as dyskinesias. These CNS side effects contrast with typical Parkinsonian symptoms, indicating excessive dopamine activity at basal ganglia receptors. Levodopa may also result in mood changes, depression, psychosis, and anxiety.

Interactions: The vitamin pyridoxine (B6) increases the peripheral breakdown of levodopa, reducing its effectiveness. When levodopa is taken alongside monoamine oxidase inhibitors (MAOIs) like phenelzine, it can lead to a hypertensive crisis due to heightened catecholamine production. Therefore, caution is necessary when these medications are used together.

In psychotic patients, levodopa may worsen symptoms by increasing central catecholamine levels. In patients with glaucoma, it can elevate intraocular pressure. Cardiac patients need careful monitoring due to the potential for arrhythmias. Antipsychotic drugs are usually contraindicated for Parkinsonian patients since they block dopamine receptors and may induce Parkinsonian symptoms themselves. However, low doses of certain "atypical" antipsychotic agents may be prescribed to manage levodopa-induced psychiatric symptoms.

Selegiline and Rasagiline

Selegiline (also known as deprenyl) selectively inhibits monoamine oxidase Type B (MAO-B), which breaks down dopamine at low to moderate doses. It does not affect monoamine oxidase Type A (MAO-A), which metabolizes norepinephrine and serotonin unless taken in excessive doses. By reducing dopamine metabolism, selegiline increases dopamine levels in the brain, thereby enhancing the effects of levodopa and reducing the required levodopa dosage. Unlike nonselective MAOIs, selegiline at recommended doses poses minimal risk for hypertensive crises. However, at high doses, it loses selectivity and may lead to severe hypertension. Selegiline is metabolized into methamphetamine and amphetamine, which can cause insomnia if taken later in the day. Rasagiline is a more potent, irreversible, and selective inhibitor of brain MAO-B, being five times stronger than selegiline. Unlike selegiline, rasagiline does not produce amphetamine-like metabolites.

Catechol-O-Methyltransferase Inhibitors

Typically, levodopa is metabolized through a minor pathway by catechol-O-methyltransferase (COMT), converting it to 3-O-methyldopa. However, when carbidopa inhibits peripheral dopamine decarboxylase activity, a significant amount of 3-O-methyldopa is produced, which competes with levodopa for transport into the central nervous system (CNS).

Inhibiting COMT with drugs like entacapone or tolcapone reduces plasma levels of 3-O-methyldopa, enhances levodopa uptake in the brain, and increases brain dopamine levels. Both agents have been shown to alleviate the "wearing-off" phenomena experienced by patients on levodopa-carbidopa therapy. Entacapone and tolcapone are nitrocatechol derivatives that selectively and reversibly inhibit COMT, with the primary differences lying in their pharmacokinetics and some adverse effects.

Adverse Effects

Both entacapone and tolcapone can cause side effects like diarrhea, postural hypotension, nausea, anorexia, dyskinesias, hallucinations, and sleep disturbances. Tolcapone carries a risk of severe liver damage and should only be used with liver function monitoring in patients unresponsive to other treatments. Entacapone, which lacks this toxicity, has largely replaced tolcapone.

Dopamine-Receptor Agonists

This group includes bromocriptine, ropinirole, pramipexole, and rotigotine. These medications have a longer duration of action than levodopa and are effective for patients with motor fluctuations. They present a lower risk of dyskinesias when used as initial therapy. However, they are ineffective in patients who do not respond to levodopa. Apomorphine is used as an injectable dopamine agonist for severe and advanced Parkinson's disease stages.

Drugs Used in Alzheimer's

Definition

Alzheimer's disease is a progressive neurodegenerative disorder characterized by memory loss, cognitive decline, and behavioral changes. It is marked by the accumulation of amyloid plaques and neurofibrillary tangles in the brain, leading to impaired daily functioning and eventual loss of independence.

Classification of Drugs for Alzheimer's Disease

I. Cholinesterase Inhibitors

(a) Donepezil
(b) Rivastigmine
(c) Galantamine

II. NMDA Receptor Antagonist

(a) Memantine

Cholinesterase Inhibitors

Cholinesterase inhibitors are the first-line treatment for mild to moderate Alzheimer's disease. They work by increasing levels of acetylcholine, a neurotransmitter associated with memory and learning, by inhibiting the enzyme that breaks it down.

Mechanism of Action

Cholinesterase inhibitors block the enzyme acetylcholinesterase, which breaks down acetylcholine in the synaptic cleft. This action enhances cholinergic transmission in the brain, potentially improving cognitive function and slowing disease progression.

Actions

These medications help to improve memory, cognitive function, and overall quality of life in individuals with Alzheimer's disease.

Therapeutic Uses

Cholinesterase inhibitors are effective in managing symptoms of mild to moderate Alzheimer's disease. They may provide symptomatic relief and lead to a modest improvement in cognitive function and daily living activities.

Absorption and Metabolism

Cholinesterase inhibitors are well absorbed after oral administration. Donepezil has a long half-life, allowing for once-daily dosing, while rivastigmine and galantamine may require multiple doses due to shorter half-lives.

Adverse Effects

Common side effects include gastrointestinal issues (nausea, vomiting, diarrhea), insomnia, muscle cramps, and bradycardia. These effects arise from increased cholinergic activity in the body.

NMDA Receptor Antagonist

Memantine is used in moderate to severe Alzheimer's disease and acts on glutamatergic pathways.

Mechanism of Action

Memantine is a non-competitive antagonist of the NMDA receptor, which regulates glutamate activity in the brain. It helps prevent excitotoxicity, a process that can lead to neuronal damage.

Actions

Memantine helps to improve or stabilize cognitive function and may reduce behavioral symptoms associated with Alzheimer's disease.

Therapeutic Uses

It is primarily used to treat moderate to severe Alzheimer's disease, often in conjunction with cholinesterase inhibitors for enhanced effect.

Absorption and Metabolism

Memantine is absorbed rapidly and is primarily excreted unchanged in the urine. It has a half-life of about 60 to 80 hours, allowing for once-daily dosing.

Adverse Effects

Side effects may include dizziness, headache, confusion, constipation, and hypertension. These effects are generally mild and may improve with continued use.

8.2 ANTIEPILEPTIC DRUGS

About 10% of the population experiences at least one seizure during their lifetime. Worldwide, epilepsy ranks as the fourth most prevalent neurological disorder, following migraine, cerebrovascular diseases (such as stroke), and Alzheimer's disease. Rather than being a single condition, epilepsy encompasses various seizure types and syndromes that arise from different underlying mechanisms, all characterized by sudden, excessive, and synchronous discharges of neurons in the brain. This abnormal electrical activity can lead to a range of symptoms, including loss of consciousness, unusual movements, odd behavior, and distorted perceptions, which are typically brief but can recur if left untreated. The specific symptoms depend on the area of the brain where the abnormal neuronal firing originates. For instance, seizures beginning in the motor cortex may lead to abnormal movements or generalized convulsions, while those originating in the parietal or occipital lobe can result in visual, auditory, or olfactory hallucinations. The primary treatment for epilepsy is medication, and about 75% of patients can manage their seizures effectively with a single drug. However, some patients may need multiple medications for optimal seizure control, and a portion may never achieve complete control over their seizures.

Etiology of Seizures

Epilepsy can arise from various underlying causes, including genetic, structural, or metabolic factors, or it may have no identifiable cause at all. In many instances, the cause of epilepsy remains unknown. The neuronal discharges associated with epilepsy originate from a small group of neurons in a specific brain region known as the "primary focus." Functionally abnormal focal areas can be triggered into activity by physiological changes such as variations in blood gases, pH levels, electrolytes, and blood glucose, as well as environmental factors like sleep deprivation, alcohol consumption, and stress. Certain triggers, including illicit drug use, tumors, head injuries, hypoglycemia, meningeal infections, and rapid withdrawal from alcohol, can provoke seizures. If a seizure has a specific, identifiable cause that can be addressed, medication may not be necessary. For example, a seizure resulting from a drug reaction does not qualify as epilepsy and does not require ongoing treatment. Conversely, antiseizure medications, also known as antiepileptic drugs (AEDs), may be necessary when the underlying cause of the seizures cannot be corrected.

CLASSIFICATION OF SEIZURES

Accurate classification of seizures is crucial for determining the appropriate treatment. Seizures can be categorized based on their origin, underlying causes, electrophysiological characteristics, and clinical presentation. The classification system established by the International League Against Epilepsy is widely recognized as the standard for classifying seizures and epilepsy syndromes. Seizures fall into two main categories: focal and generalized.

A. **Focal Seizures:** Focal seizures affect only a specific part of one hemisphere of the brain. The symptoms vary depending on where the neuronal activity occurs and how much it spreads to other neurons. Focal seizures can progress to bilateral tonic-clonic seizures, and patients may experience loss of consciousness or awareness. These seizures can start with either motor or nonmotor symptoms.

B. Generalized Seizures: Generalized seizures often begin in a localized area but then spread to involve abnormal electrical activity across both hemispheres of the brain. Primary generalized seizures can be either convulsive or nonconvulsive, with immediate loss of consciousness in most cases.

1. **Tonic-clonic seizures** lead to loss of consciousness, followed by a tonic phase (sustained muscle contraction) and a clonic phase (rapid muscle contractions and relaxations). Afterward, patients may experience confusion and fatigue due to depleted glucose and energy reserves.
2. **Absence seizures** result in a brief and sudden loss of consciousness, typically starting in children aged 3 to 5 and lasting until puberty or longer. During an absence seizure, the patient stares blankly and may blink rapidly for 3 to 5 seconds. Electroencephalograms (EEGs) reveal a characteristic three-per-second spike and wave pattern.
3. **Myoclonic seizures** consist of short bursts of muscle contractions that can occur repeatedly over several minutes. They usually happen after waking up and are present as quick jerks of the limbs. Myoclonic seizures can begin at any age but typically start around puberty or early adulthood.
4. **Clonic seizures** involve brief episodes of muscle contractions that closely resemble myoclonic seizures, but there is usually a greater impairment of consciousness.
5. **Tonic seizures** are characterized by increased muscle tone, primarily in the extensor muscles, usually lasting less than 60 seconds.
6. **Atonic seizures**, also referred to as drop attacks, are marked by a sudden loss of muscle tone.

Classification

First-Generation AEDs

- Phenobarbital
- Primidone
- Phenytoin
- Ethosuximide
- Carbamazepine
- Valproic Acid

Second-Generation AEDs

- Felbamate
- Gabapentin
- Lamotrigine
- Topiramate
- Tiagabine
- Levetiracetam
- Oxcarbazepine
- Zonisamide
- Pregabalin

Newest Drugs

- Rufinamide
- Stiripentol
- Lacosamide
- Retigabine
- Eslicarbazepine
- Perampanel

C. **Mechanism of Action of Antiseizure Medications:** The development of a seizure involves various structures and processes, including neurons, ion channels, receptors, glial cells, and both inhibitory and excitatory synapses. Antiepileptic drugs (AEDs) are specifically designed to modify these mechanisms.

Mechanisms of Action of Antiseizure Medications

Antiseizure medications (AEDs) promote inhibition over excitation in the brain to stop or prevent seizure activity. Narrow-spectrum AEDs are effective for specific types of seizures, such as focal or absence seizures, while broad-spectrum AEDs can address a wider range of seizures, including both partial and absent myoclonic seizures. These drugs reduce seizures through various mechanisms, such as blocking voltage-gated sodium (Na^+) or calcium (Ca^{2+}) channels, enhancing inhibitory signals from γ-aminobutyric acid (GABA), and interfering with excitatory glutamate transmission. Some AEDs target multiple pathways within the central nervous system (CNS), while the mechanisms of action for certain medications remain less understood. Although AEDs can suppress seizures effectively, they do not cure or prevent epilepsy.

DRUG SELECTION

The selection of AEDs is guided by the type of seizures, patient-specific factors (such as age, existing medical conditions, lifestyle, and personal preferences), and the characteristics of the medications (including cost and potential drug interactions). For instance, different medications are used to treat focal-onset seizures compared to primary generalized seizures, although there is some overlap in effective agents. Toxicity and individual patient characteristics play significant roles in drug selection. In newly diagnosed patients, treatment typically starts with a single medication, which is gradually increased until seizures are controlled or side effects occur. It is advisable to avoid changing AEDs if seizures are well managed. Patients on monotherapy generally show better adherence to their medication and experience fewer side effects compared to those on combination therapy. If seizures remain uncontrolled with the initial medication, the next step may be to switch to a different monotherapy or consider a combination of medications.

Addition of Medications

When considering the addition of medications for seizure management, the following prescribing guidelines should be followed:

- If the initial AED was only partially effective, it should be continued until the new AED reaches therapeutic levels.
- If seizures are controlled, consider tapering off the initial medication.
- Switch to another AED if the first drug is ineffective or not well tolerated.
- Gradually withdraw any AEDs that are ineffective.
- Avoid prescribing more than three AEDs at a time.
- Emphasize the importance of regular AED usage to prevent loss of seizure control before starting treatment and assess adherence at each follow-up visit.
- Review the diagnosis to confirm it is a true seizure in patients not responding to treatment.
- The goal of therapy is complete seizure freedom with a single first-line AED taken once or twice a day, with minimal side effects.

Understanding the available antiseizure medications, their mechanisms of action, pharmacokinetics, potential drug interactions, and adverse effects is crucial for successful treatment. Physiological differences among neonates, infants, children, and adults can influence the absorption, distribution, metabolism, and excretion of AEDs. These pharmacokinetic variations may contribute to age-related differences in the incidence of adverse effects, necessitating careful dose selection and monitoring. Children on AEDs should be regularly followed up for compliance, seizure recurrence, and side effects. It's important to monitor their growth and adjust doses accordingly. If medication adjustments are insufficient, consider other treatment options, such as vagal nerve stimulation or surgery.

Therapeutic Drug Monitoring

Therapeutic drug monitoring (TDM) for AEDs aims to optimize patient outcomes by managing medication regimens based on the concentration of AEDs in serum or plasma. Identifying the optimal dose for an individual based solely on clinical presentation can be challenging; therefore, TDM is necessary in the following situations:

1. **Prescribed Dosage**: Since AED treatment is preventive and seizures occur unpredictably, it can be difficult to quickly ascertain whether the prescribed dosage will effectively control seizures in the long term.
2. **Clinical Symptoms**: Signs of toxicity can be subtle or hard to differentiate from symptoms of underlying disorders.
3. **Laboratory Markers**: There are no direct laboratory markers for assessing clinical efficacy or the common signs of AED toxicity, such as adverse effects on the central nervous system (CNS).

However, routine monitoring of AED blood levels is not generally necessary; "routine" drug level checks are not recommended for controlled, non-toxic patients.

Discontinuing Antiepileptic Drugs

Treatment for epilepsy typically lasts for 2 to 3 years, although the duration can vary based on the cause and type of seizures. Stopping antiepileptic drugs (AEDs) abruptly is risky and can lead to the return of seizures or even prolonged seizures, known as status epilepticus. Therefore, AED withdrawal should be gradual, with the dose tapering over a period of 3 to 6 months or longer, depending on the specific medication and dosage. In particular, benzodiazepines and barbiturates should be withdrawn very slowly due to the risk of withdrawal seizures.

Antiseizure Medications

The Food and Drug Administration (FDA) has approved many new antiseizure medications in recent decades. Some of these newer agents may offer advantages over older drugs in terms of pharmacokinetics, tolerability, and a lower risk of drug interactions. However, studies have not consistently shown that these newer medications are significantly more effective than their older counterparts.

A. Benzodiazepines

Benzodiazepines work by binding to GABA-inhibitory receptors, reducing the rate of neuronal firing. They are primarily used for emergency or acute seizure treatment due to the development of tolerance over time. However, clonazepam and clobazam may be prescribed as adjunctive therapy for specific seizure types. Diazepam is available for rectal administration to manage prolonged generalized tonic-clonic seizures or clusters when oral administration is not feasible.

B. Brivaracetam

Brivaracetam is approved for treating focal-onset seizures in adults. It has a high and selective affinity for a synaptic vesicle protein (SV2A), although its exact mechanism of action is still unknown. The drug is well absorbed when taken orally and is metabolized through hydrolysis and CYP2C19 (to a lesser extent). Co-administration with strong CYP-inducing medications can lower plasma concentrations of brivaracetam. Additionally, it is a moderate inhibitor of epoxide hydrolase, which may increase levels of the active metabolite of carbamazepine when taken together.

C. Carbamazepine

Carbamazepine works by blocking sodium channels, which may help inhibit the generation of repetitive action potentials in neurons. Carbamazepine is typically maintained at a dose of 200 mg/day for complete seizure control. It functions as an inducer of various cytochrome P450 enzymes, specifically CYP1A2, CYP2C, CYP3A, and UDP glucuronosyltransferase (UGT), which can increase the clearance of other drugs. Common side effects of carbamazepine include:

- **Diplopia**
- **Headache**
- **Dizziness**
- **Nausea**
- **Vomiting**

Some of these adverse effects may arise from its active epoxide metabolite. Patients may experience peak-related side effects around 2 hours after dosing, necessitating administration three or four times daily for some individuals. Switching to a controlled-release formulation, which can be administered twice daily, may help alleviate these peak dose-related side effects.

Idiosyncratic Reactions

Carbamazepine can cause various idiosyncratic reactions, with skin rash being the most common. A slow titration of the dosage can help mitigate this risk. In rare instances, it may lead to severe skin reactions, such as:

- **Erythema multiforme**
- **Stevens-Johnson syndrome** (a dermatological emergency)

Mild leucopenia may occur and is typically reversible with no clinical significance. At elevated levels, carbamazepine may exhibit an antidiuretic hormone-like effect, causing fluid retention, particularly in elderly patients with cardiac failure. While mild hyponatremia is usually asymptomatic, serum sodium levels falling below 125 mmol/L can result in confusion, peripheral edema, and worsening seizure control. Cardiac arrhythmias are also potential complications of carbamazepine therapy.

Cautions

Carbamazepine is contraindicated in patients with absence seizures, as it may exacerbate these seizures. Notably, carbamazepine is a strong enzyme inducer, leading to autoinduction and accelerating the clearance of numerous lipid-soluble drugs, including hormonal contraceptives. This necessitates a higher daily estrogen dose for many women on the contraceptive pill.

Affected medications include:

- **Sodium valproate**
- **Ethosuximide**
- **Corticosteroids**
- **Anticoagulants**
- **Antipsychotics**
- **Cyclosporin**

Drugs that may inhibit carbamazepine metabolism, increasing the risk of toxicity, include:

- **Phenytoin**
- **Isoniazid**
- **Cimetidine**
- **Danazol**
- **Dextropropoxyphene**
- **Erythromycin**

- **Verapamil**
- **Diltiazem**
- **Viloxazine**

D. Oxcarbazepine

Oxcarbazepine is a prodrug that rapidly converts to its active metabolite, the 10-monohydroxy derivative (MHD), which is responsible for its anticonvulsant effects. MHD blocks sodium channels and may also modulate calcium channels. Oxcarbazepine is approved for use in adults and children for focal seizures. It is a less potent inducer of CYP3A4 and UGT compared to carbamazepine. However, the adverse effect of hyponatremia limits its use in elderly patients.

E. Eslicarbazepine

Eslicarbazepine acetate is another prodrug that is hydrolyzed to its active metabolite, eslicarbazepine (also known as S-licarbazepine). It acts as a voltage-gated sodium channel blocker and is approved for the treatment of focal seizures in adults. Eslicarbazepine has linear pharmacokinetics and is *eliminated via glucuronidation. Its side effects include:*

- **Dizziness**
- **Somnolence**
- **Diplopia**
- **Headache**

Severe adverse reactions, such as rash, psychiatric effects, and hyponatremia, are rare.

F. Ethosuximide

Ethosuximide is primarily effective in treating absence seizures. It reduces the propagation of abnormal electrical activity in the brain, likely by inhibiting T-type calcium channels. This mechanism is particularly beneficial for managing the characteristic seizure activity associated with absence seizures.

G. Felbamate

Felbamate possesses a broad spectrum of anticonvulsant action with multiple proposed mechanisms, including:

- Blocking voltage-dependent sodium channels
- Competing with the glycine binding site on the N-methyl-d-aspartate (NMDA) glutamate receptor
- Blocking calcium channels
- Potentiating GABA action

It acts as an inhibitor for drugs metabolized by CYP2C19 and induces those metabolized by CYP3A4. Due to the risk of serious adverse effects, including aplastic anemia (approximately 1 in 4000) and hepatic failure, felbamate is reserved for use in refractory epilepsies, particularly Lennox–Gastaut syndrome.

H. Gabapentin

Gabapentin is an analog of GABA but does not interact with GABA receptors, enhance GABA actions, or convert to GABA itself. Its mechanism of action is not fully understood; however, it binds to the $\alpha 2\delta$ subunit of voltage-gated calcium channels, which may contribute to its anticonvulsant properties.

Gabapentin is approved as an adjunct therapy for focal seizures and for the treatment of postherpetic neuralgia. Notably, it exhibits nonlinear pharmacokinetics due to saturation of its gut transport system, and it does not bind to plasma proteins. Gabapentin is excreted unchanged by the kidneys, necessitating dose adjustments in patients with renal impairment.

Tolerability and Side Effects

Gabapentin is generally well tolerated, especially in the elderly population, due to its mild side effects. It does not induce hepatic enzymes and has minimal potential for drug interactions, making it a suitable option for patients at high risk for such interactions.

Common side effects associated with gabapentin include:

- **Drowsiness**
- **Dizziness**
- **Diplopia**
- **Ataxia**
- **Headaches**

At high doses, gabapentin may lead to weight gain and could occasionally exacerbate seizures, particularly myoclonic seizures. Importantly, no serious idiosyncratic reactions to gabapentin have been reported to date.

I. Lacosamide

Lacosamide is an anticonvulsant medication that primarily affects voltage-gated sodium channels, leading to the stabilization of hyperexcitable neuronal membranes and inhibition of repetitive neuronal firing. It also binds to collapsin response mediator protein-2 (CRMP-2), a phosphoprotein involved in neuronal differentiation and the regulation of axonal outgrowth. However, the specific role of CRMP-2 binding in the context of seizure control remains unclear.

Lacosamide is approved for adjunctive treatment of focal seizures. *Common adverse events that may limit its use include:*

- **Dizziness**
- **Headache**
- **Fatigue**

J. Lamotrigine

Lamotrigine is an effective anticonvulsant that blocks sodium channels as well as high-voltage-dependent calcium channels. Its broad spectrum of activity makes it suitable for treating various seizure types, including focal seizures and generalized seizures, particularly in patients with epilepsy syndromes such as Lennox-Gastaut syndrome and absence seizures.

Mechanism of Action

By inhibiting sodium channels, lamotrigine stabilizes neuronal membranes, thus reducing the likelihood of seizure activity. Its action on calcium channels further contributes to its efficacy in managing seizures.

Tolerability and Side Effects

Lamotrigine is generally well tolerated, but it may cause side effects, which can include:

- **Rash** (potentially serious, such as Stevens-Johnson syndrome)
- **Dizziness**
- **Headache**
- **Nausea**
- **Somnolence**

The risk of skin rashes can be mitigated by slow titration of the dose, especially when lamotrigine is used in combination with other antiepileptic drugs that may interact with its metabolism.

Overall, lamotrigine's favorable side effect profile, along with its efficacy, makes it a commonly prescribed option in the management of epilepsy.

Lamotrigine is used to manage a variety of seizure types, including:

- **Focal seizures**
- **Generalized seizures**
- **Absence seizures**
- **Lennox–Gastaut syndrome**

In addition to its anticonvulsant properties, lamotrigine is also employed in the treatment of bipolar disorder.

Pharmacokinetics

Lamotrigine is primarily metabolized to the 2-N-glucuronide metabolite via the UGT1A4 pathway. Its clearance can be affected by other medications:

- **General enzyme inducers** (e.g., carbamazepine) can increase lamotrigine clearance, leading to lower drug concentrations.
- **Valproate** significantly decreases lamotrigine clearance, resulting in higher drug concentrations. Consequently, when adding valproate to a regimen that includes lamotrigine, dosages of lamotrigine should be reduced to avoid toxicity.

Titration and Side Effects

Due to the potential risk of serious rashes, including Stevens-Johnson syndrome, a slow titration schedule is crucial when initiating lamotrigine therapy, especially in patients who are also taking valproate. Common side effects may include:

- **Headache**
- **Drowsiness**
- **Ataxia**
- **Diplopia**
- **Insomnia**
- **Nausea**
- **Dizziness**

These side effects are particularly prominent during dose escalation.

K. Levetiracetam

Levetiracetam is an anticonvulsant approved for adjunctive therapy in various seizure types, including:

- **Focal onset seizures**
- **Myoclonic seizures**
- **Primary generalized tonic-clonic seizures**

Mechanism of Action

Levetiracetam demonstrates a high affinity for a synaptic vesicle protein (SV2A), which is believed to play a role in neurotransmitter release. It is well absorbed after oral administration and primarily excreted unchanged in urine, resulting in minimal drug interactions.

Side Effects

While generally well tolerated, levetiracetam can cause mood alterations, which may necessitate a dose adjustment or a change in medication.

L. Perampanel

Perampanel is classified as a selective α-amino-3-hydroxy-5-methyl-4-isoxazolepropionic acid (AMPA) antagonist, which reduces excitatory neurotransmission.

Dosing and Approval

- It has a long half-life, allowing for once-daily dosing.
- Perampanel is approved for adjunctive treatment of both focal and generalized tonic-clonic seizures.

Warnings

This medication carries warnings for serious psychiatric and behavioral reactions, which may include:

- **Aggression**
- **Hostility**
- **Irritability**
- **Anger**
- **Homicidal ideation**

M. Phenobarbital and Primidone

Phenobarbital is a classic anticonvulsant that enhances GABA-mediated inhibition in the central nervous system. **Primidone** is a prodrug that is metabolized into phenobarbital and phenylethylmalonamide, both of which possess anticonvulsant activity.

Efficacy and Use

Phenobarbital remains a first-line treatment for focal and tonic-clonic seizures but is infrequently used in developed countries due to its cognitive, mood, and behavioral effects. Common side effects include:

- **Fatigue**
- **Listlessness**
- **Tiredness** (in adults)
- **Insomnia**
- **Hyperactivity** (in children)

Due to these side effects, it should be initiated at a low dose (e.g., 30 mg in adolescents and adults) and titrated gradually (e.g., increasing by 15 mg) based on clinical response, with usual therapeutic doses ranging from 60 to 120 mg per day.

Drug Interactions and Considerations

As an enzyme inducer, phenobarbital can accelerate the metabolism of various lipid-soluble drugs and may negatively impact bone health. Monitoring drug levels is of limited value due to its wide therapeutic range (15 to 45 mg/L), and the effective concentration for seizure control can vary significantly among individuals. Furthermore, patients often develop tolerance to the central nervous system side effects, complicating dose management.

N. Phenytoin and Fosphenytoin

Phenytoin is an anticonvulsant that effectively blocks voltage-gated sodium channels by selectively binding to the channel in its inactive state, thereby slowing the rate of recovery. It is commonly used for:

- **Focal seizures**
- **Generalized tonic-clonic seizures**
- **Status epilepticus**

Pharmacokinetics

Phenytoin induces the metabolism of several cytochrome P450 enzymes (CYP2C and CYP3A families) and the UGT enzyme system. It exhibits saturable enzyme metabolism, which results in nonlinear pharmacokinetics. This means that small increases in the daily dose can lead to disproportionately large increases in plasma concentration, increasing the risk of drug-induced toxicity.

- **Saturable Kinetics**: Phenytoin is one of the few medications that switch from first-order kinetics (where the rate of elimination is proportional to the drug concentration) to zero-order kinetics (where the rate of elimination is constant) at therapeutic dosages. This can lead to unexpected rises in drug levels and subsequent neurotoxicity if the dose is increased slightly.
- **Therapeutic Range**: Phenytoin has a narrow therapeutic range (10 to 20 mmol/L). Levels above this range can result in neurotoxic symptoms, including drowsiness, dysarthria, tremor, ataxia, and cognitive difficulties. Importantly, diagnosis of toxicity should be made clinically rather than solely based on plasma levels.

Side Effects

Common adverse effects associated with phenytoin include:

- **CNS Depression**: Particularly affecting the cerebellum and vestibular system, leading to symptoms like nystagmus and ataxia. The elderly is especially vulnerable.
- **Cosmetic Changes**: Reversible effects such as gum hyperplasia, acne, hirsutism, and facial coarsening. Gingival hyperplasia can lead to significant overgrowth of the gums over teeth.
- **Long-term Risks**: Prolonged use may lead to peripheral neuropathies and osteoporosis.
- **Cerebellar Damage**: Chronic toxicity may cause permanent cerebellar damage, which can manifest as mental slowing and unsteadiness, with neurological examinations showing cerebellar signs.

Drug Interactions

Phenytoin can accelerate the metabolism of other lipid-soluble drugs, including:

- **Carbamazepine**
- **Sodium valproate**
- **Ethosuximide**
- **Anticoagulants**
- **Steroids**
- **Cyclosporin**

Displacement interactions related to protein binding are only clinically significant in the presence of concurrent enzyme inhibition, notably when phenytoin is combined with sodium valproate.

Fosphenytoin is a prodrug that rapidly converts to phenytoin in the bloodstream. It can be administered intramuscularly (IM), unlike phenytoin sodium, which should never be given IM due to the risk of tissue damage and necrosis. Fosphenytoin is the preferred choice for IV and IM administration of phenytoin.

O. Pregabalin

Pregabalin is an anticonvulsant that binds to the $\alpha 2\delta$ subunit of voltage-gated calcium channels in the central nervous system (CNS).

Mechanism of Action

By binding to this site, pregabalin inhibits excitatory neurotransmitter release, thereby reducing neuronal excitability. It is effective for:

- **Focal seizures**
- **Neuropathic pain**
- **Generalized anxiety disorder**
- **Fibromyalgia**

Pharmacokinetics

Pregabalin is well absorbed after oral administration and is not significantly metabolized, leading to predictable pharmacokinetics. It is primarily excreted unchanged in urine.

Side Effects

Common side effects of pregabalin include:

- **Dizziness**
- **Drowsiness**
- **Peripheral edema**
- **Weight gain**

Because of its sedation potential, care should be taken when initiating therapy, particularly in elderly patients or those taking other CNS depressants. Pregabalin has a favorable side effect profile compared to older anticonvulsants, making it a useful option in the management of seizures and neuropathic pain immediate medical attention. The management of status epilepticus involves the rapid administration of antiepileptic drugs (AEDs) to prevent neuronal damage and restore normal neurological function.

Initial Management

1. **Stabilization**
   - Ensure the patient's airway is clear, provide supplemental oxygen if needed, and establish intravenous access.
   - Monitor vital signs and assess for potential complications.
2. **Benzodiazepines**
   - **Lorazepam (Ativan)**: The first-line treatment due to its rapid onset and prolonged effect. Typically given as an intravenous bolus (4 mg over 2 minutes) with a repeat dose after 10-15 minutes if seizures continue.
     - **Diazepam (Valium)**: Can also be used but has a shorter duration of action and may lead to less effective seizure control if repeated doses are required, administered intravenously or rectally.

- **Midazolam**: An alternative for patients who cannot receive intravenous medications.

3. **Loading Dose of Antiepileptic Drugs**
   - After the initial benzodiazepine treatment, a loading dose of a longer-acting AED is often required. Options include:

- **Phenytoin**: Administered slowly IV (usually 15-20 mg/kg) to prevent hypotension and cardiac arrhythmias.
- **Fosphenytoin**: A prodrug of phenytoin that can be administered more rapidly and can be given IM or IV.
- **Valproic acid**: Effective in both generalized and focal seizures and can be administered intravenously.
- **Levetiracetam**: Another option that can be given IV and has a favorable side effect profile.
- **Lacosamide**: Also used in status epilepticus, typically given as an IV loading dose.

4. **Refractory Status Epilepticus**
   - If seizures persist despite treatment with benzodiazepines and a loading dose of an AED, the status is considered refractory. The following strategies may be employed:

- **Continuous infusion of anesthetics**, such as propofol or pentobarbital, can be used to induce a coma to stop seizures.
- **Additional AEDs**: Consider adding other medications like phenobarbital, topiramate, or zonisamide.
- **General anesthesia**: This may be needed in severe cases to control seizures.

Monitoring and Supportive Care

- G are in place to prevent injury during seizures.

Conclusion

Prompt recognition and aggressive management of status epilepticus are crucial to prevent complications such as neuronal injury or permanent disability. Continuous assessment of the patient's response to treatment and adjustment of medications is essential to achieving seizure control and ensuring the best possible outcomes.n

CHAPTER 9

Cognitive and Memory Enhancement

9.1 COGNITIVE ENHANCERS OR NOOTROPICS

Cognition enhancers are drugs which help to reduce the impairment of cognitive functions associated with age, head injury, stroke and neurodegenerative disorders.

Nootropics can overcome or retard cognitive decline occurring in old age and in some diseased conditions. They can prevent the disruption of the process of memory consolidation by hypoxia, trauma, seizures, hypoglycaemia, and other aversive factors. Nootropics should possess the following properties: They should facilitate learning acquisition and memory consolidation and prevent or mitigate impairment of memory induced by ageing, amnestic agents and other aversive factors and facilitate inter-hemispheric transfer of information.

They belong to diverse chemical categories. Some of them are listed below:

Piracetam and its congeners: Aniracetam, Oxiracetam.

Hydergine (dihydroergotoxin)

Vincamine

Meclofenoxate

Pentoxifylline

Pyritinol

Cyclangate

Nicergoline

Herpestis monniera (Brahmi)

Ginkgo biloba extract

Mechanism of Action

Nootropics like Pentoxifylline, Pyritinol, Cyclandate and Nicergoline function like cerebral protectors improving cerebral circulation. The actions of other drugs are more complex. Improve brain metabolism and energy utilisation may be involved, as well as effects on central neurotransmitters. There is evidence that central cholinergic synapses may be part of the intrinsic system controlling memory storage. Nootropics may induce an environment of neurotransmitters conducive to learning acquisition and memory retention. The mechanism of action includes an increase in central cholinergic, noradrenergic, and dopaminergic activity with concomitant reduction in serotonergic function.

Piracetam

Piracetam is a cyclised derivative of GABA. It was first introduced as a nootropic agent. It has been shown to be beneficial in cognitive deficits occurring in several types of brain disorders. Mental performance is improved in children and ageing individuals with memory deficits. Piracetam is devoid of significant autonomic, motor, or behavioural effects, even at relatively high doses. Piracetam has been proposed to augment energy utilisation and increase resistance to adverse cellular changes induced by anoxia. Changes induced by Piracetam on central neurotransmitters may also contribute to its nootropic action. Aniracetam and Oxiracetam are derivatives of Piracetam. The dose of Piracetam is 2-3 gm daily in divided doses.

Therapeutic Uses

- In cognitive defects associated with personality (Alzheimer's disease) and ageing.
- In children with learning and attention deficits.
- Amnesia following cerebral trauma, drug abuse including alcoholism, and seizures.
- Coexisting memory deficits in neurological and psychiatric illnesses.

9.2 CNS STIMULANTS

These are drugs whose primary action is to stimulate the CNS globally or to improve specific brain functions. The CNS stimulants mostly produce a generalised action, which may, at high doses, result in convulsions. Given below is a working classification based primarily on the clinical use, because clear cut differences do not exist.

Classification

The drugs in this category have a marked influence on mental functions and behaviour to produce excitement, euphoria, increase in motor activity and reduction in fatigue. They are sub-classified as follows:

1. **Amphetamines/non-amphetamines**
   - **Amphetamine group:** e.g. Amphetamine, Dexaamphetamine, Methamphetamine, Methylenedioxy methamphetamine (MDMA), Methylphenidate and Fenfluramine.
   - **Non-amphetamine group:** e.g. Modafinil, Atomoxetine, Sibutramine and Pemoline.
2. **Methylxanthines**

   The pharmacological effects of amphetamines and non-amphetamines are almost the same. Hence, only methylxanthines are discussed separately.

Amphetamines/non-amphetamines

Mechanism of Action

Drugs enter the nerve ending

↓

Active transport of drugs into storage vesicles

↓

Drug alter the pH of storage vesicles

↓

Displacement of DA/NE from storage vesicles

↓

Inhibition of DA metabolism

↓

Drug inhibit MAO-B in the nerve ending

↓

Increase DA concentration in the synaptic cleft.

Pharmacological Effects

The following are the main central effects of Amphetamine-like drugs:

- Increased motor activity
- Euphoria and excitement
- Anorexia
- Stereotyped and psychotic behaviour with prolonged administration.
- Rise in BP and inhibition of GIT motility.
- Increase the wakefulness, capacity to work and euphoria. Hence, there is unawareness of fatigue, which can be dangerous.

Pharmacokinetics

All these drugs are well absorbed orally and freely penetrate BBB. A considerable portion of the un metabolised drug is excreted through urine. It is possible to trap this weakly basic drug by acidifying urine with ascorbic acid or ammonium chloride. Acidification reduces its absorption from renal tubules and enhances its clearance.

Clinical Uses

- Attention deficit hyperkinetic disorder (ADHD) with minimal brain dysfunction
- Narcolepsy
- Appetite suppression

Methyl-Xanthines

The popularity of xanthine-containing drinks such as coffee, tea and coke appear to be related to their CNS-stimulating effects.

Xanthine derivatives are: Caffeine, Theobromine, Theophylline and its derivatives like Aminophylline, Etophylline, Acebrophylline and Enprophylline.

Theophylline is found in tea, Theobromine in coca while caeffine is found in coffee, tea and cola drinks.

Mechanism of Action

Methylxanthines

↓

Inhibit phosphodiesterase (PDE)

↓

Increased 3', 5' - cyclic AMP Concentration

↓

Bronchodilation

↓

Inhibit cell surface adenosine receptors

↓

Antagonize adenosine effects (Drowsiness, motor incoordination, cerebral vasodilation, CNS depression, anticonvulsant action, bronchoconstiction)

↓

Enhance deacetylation of histones

↓

Prevent transcription of inflammatory genes

↓

Anti-inflammatory action

Pharmacological Actions

1. **CNS effects:** They act as CNS stimulants. The rank order is caeffine > Theophylline > Theobromine. CNS stimulation causes wakefulness, alertness, and increased capacity to do intellectual work with better association of ideas. They produce equal fatigue reduction much less locomotor stimulation, but produce no euphoria, stereotyped behaviour, or psychotic manifestations.
2. **CVS effects:** They produce an increase in heart rate peripheral vasodilation. BP is not affected. Cardiac output is increased, which is an advantage in CHF patients. Coronary blood flow is increased. Cranial blood vessels are constricted; oxygen tension in the brain is reduced. Caffeine is useful in migraine.

3. **Kidney:** They are mild diuretics, but the action is brief. The action is due to increased filtration pressure at the glomerulus and due to increased cardiac output.
4. **Miscellaneous effects:** They stimulate the medullary respiratory centre, bronchodilation. biliary spasm is reduced, facilitating neuromuscular transmission by increasing the release of ACh and enhancing the contractile power of skeletal muscles, increasing gastric acid and pepsin secretion leading to gastric irritation.
5. **Theophylline inhibits:** the release of histamine and other mediators in mast cells. This is the basis of their action in bronchial asthma.

Clinical Uses

Caffeine is combined with aspirin for the treatment of headache. It is also combined with ergot alkaloids for the treatment of migraine. Oral Theophylline is used to treat COPD and mild to moderate asthma. Caffeine citrate or Theophylline is used for short-term management of apnoea in premature infants in the first few weeks of life. Aminophylline is useful in relieving paroxysmal dyspnoea, which is associated with ventricular failure.

Adverse Effects

Theophylline has a narrow margin of safety, with 8-15 μg/ml as the optimum plasma level. Above 15 μg/ml, the adverse effects are dyspepsia, headache, insomnia, restlessness, vomiting, palpitations, agitation, tachypnoea, flushing, hypotension, extra-systoles, arrhythmias, delirium, convulsions, coma leading to death. Children are more prone to toxicity.

Drug Interactions

Agents which decrease Theophylline concentration are Smoking, Phenytoin, Carbamazepine, Rifampin, and Phenobarbital.

Drugs which inhibit Theophylline metabolism are Erythromycin, Ciprofloxacin, Cimetidine, Oral contraceptives, and Allopurinol. The dose of Theophylline is to be reduced when used in combination with the mentioned drugs.

Theophylline enhances the effects of sympathomimetics, Digitalis, Furosemide, Hypoglycemic agents, and Oral anticoagulants.

Abuse of Xanthenes

Caffeine-containing beverages cause habituation but no dependence. Chronic coffee drinkers suffer from headaches and a feeling of fatigue after sudden abstention. Tolerance to these drugs is not severe.

CHAPTER 10

Future Directions and Challenges of Neuropharmacology

10.1 FUTURE OF NEUROPHARMACOLOGY RESEARCH

The future of neuropharmacology research holds tremendous promise, driven by advancements in technology, understanding of brain function, and innovative therapeutic approaches. Here are some key aspects shaping its trajectory:

Precision Medicine: With the advent of personalized medicine and advancements in genomics, neuropharmacology is moving towards tailoring treatments based on individual genetic makeup, neural circuitry, and biomarkers. This approach allows for more effective and targeted interventions with fewer side effects.

Neuroplasticity and Neuro regeneration: Research into neuroplasticity the brain's ability to reorganize itself by forming new neural connections and neuro regeneration is opening new avenues for treating neurodegenerative diseases, stroke, and spinal cord injuries. Neuropharmacology plays a crucial role in developing drugs and therapies that promote repair and recovery processes in the brain and nervous system.

Psychedelic-Assisted Therapy: There's a resurgence of interest in psychedelics such as psilocybin, MDMA, and LSD for treating mental health disorders like depression, PTSD, and addiction. Neuropharmacological research is exploring the mechanisms of action of these substances and their therapeutic potential, leading to the development of novel treatments and therapeutic protocols.

Neuroinflammation and Immune Modulation: Growing evidence suggests that neuroinflammation plays a significant role in various neurological and psychiatric disorders. Neuropharmacologists are investigating immunomodulatory drugs and interventions to regulate inflammation in the brain, offering new avenues for treating conditions like Alzheimer's disease, multiple sclerosis, and depression.

Brain-Computer Interfaces (BCIs): BCIs are revolutionizing the field of neuropharmacology by enabling direct communication between the brain and external devices. Researchers are exploring the combined use of pharmacological agents and BCI technologies to enhance cognitive function, treat neurological disorders, and restore lost sensory or motor functions.

Artificial Intelligence and Drug Discovery: AI-driven approaches are accelerating the drug discovery process in neuropharmacology by predicting drug-target interactions, designing novel compounds, and optimizing treatment regimens. Machine learning algorithms analyze large datasets to identify potential drug candidates and optimize therapeutic strategies tailored to individual patients.

Ethical and Societal Implications: As neuropharmacology advances, it raises important ethical, social, and regulatory considerations regarding the use of cognitive enhancers, neuro technologies, and psychedelic substances. Research in this field must navigate these complexities to ensure responsible and equitable access to emerging treatments while addressing concerns related to safety, equity, and unintended consequences.

Neuroinflammation Modulation: Chronic neuroinflammation is implicated in various neurological disorders, including Alzheimer's disease, Parkinson's disease, and multiple sclerosis. Advanced research in neuropharmacology focuses on developing drugs that target inflammatory pathways in the brain, such as cytokines, microglia, and astrocytes, to attenuate neuroinflammation and potentially halt disease progression.

Neuro epigenetics: Epigenetic mechanisms regulate gene expression without altering the DNA sequence and play a critical role in brain development, synaptic plasticity, and the pathogenesis of neurological disorders. Neuropharmacologists are exploring the epigenetic modifications underlying brain function and dysfunction, identifying novel drug targets and therapeutic strategies for conditions like schizophrenia, autism spectrum disorders, and addiction.

Gut-Brain Axis: The bidirectional communication between the gut microbiota and the brain, known as the gut-brain axis, influences various aspects of neurobiology, including mood, cognition, and behavior. Advanced neuropharmacology research investigates how gut microbial metabolites, neurotransmitters, and immune signaling pathways modulate brain function and mental health, with implications for developing psychobiotics and microbiota-targeted therapies for psychiatric disorders.

Neuroimmunology: The intersection of neuroscience and immunology, neuroimmunology explores the dynamic interactions between the nervous and immune systems in health and disease. Advanced neuropharmacological approaches aim to modulate immune responses in the central nervous system, harnessing immunomodulatory drugs, monoclonal antibodies, and cell-based therapies to treat neuroinflammatory conditions, neurodegenerative diseases, and brain tumors.

Nanotechnology in Drug Delivery: Nanotechnology offers innovative solutions for targeted drug delivery to the central nervous system, overcoming the blood-brain barrier and enhancing drug efficacy while minimizing systemic side effects. Advanced neuropharmacology utilizes nanocarriers, such as liposomes, nanoparticles, and exosomes, to deliver therapeutics for brain tumors, neurodegenerative disorders, and neurological infections, enabling precise and sustained drug release at the desired site of action.

Neurotransmitter Systems: Advancements in understanding the role of neurotransmitter systems such as dopamine, serotonin, glutamate, and GABA (gamma-aminobutyric acid) in brain function and dysfunction drive research in neuropharmacology. Advanced studies focus on elucidating the molecular mechanisms of neurotransmission, receptor signaling, and synaptic plasticity, informing the development of novel pharmacological agents for treating mood disorders, psychosis, and substance abuse.

Neurodegeneration and Neuroprotection: Neuropharmacological research seeks to unravel the underlying mechanisms of neurodegenerative diseases, including Alzheimer's, Parkinson's, and Huntington's disease, and identify neuroprotective strategies to preserve neuronal function and viability. Advanced approaches involve targeting protein misfolding, oxidative stress, mitochondrial dysfunction, and excitotoxicity pathways, as well as exploring neurotrophic factors and stem cell-based therapies to promote neuronal survival and regeneration.

Overall, the future of neuropharmacology research is characterized by interdisciplinary collaboration, technological innovation, and a deeper understanding of brain function, paving the way for transformative treatments and interventions for neurological and psychiatric disorders.

10.2 GENE THERAPY FOR NEUROLOGICAL DISORDERS

Gene therapy holds significant promise for treating neurological disorders by targeting underlying genetic abnormalities, restoring dysfunctional pathways, or providing neuroprotection. Here are some key notes on gene therapy for neurological disorders:

Targeted Gene Delivery: Gene therapy involves the delivery of therapeutic genes into specific cells or tissues to correct genetic defects or modulate cellular functions. Various delivery systems, including viral vectors (e.g., adeno-associated viruses, lentiviruses) and non-viral vectors (e.g., liposomes, nanoparticles), are utilized to efficiently and selectively transfer genes into neurons or glial cells within the central nervous system (CNS).

Monogenic Disorders: Gene therapy has shown promise in treating monogenic neurological disorders caused by mutations in a single gene. For example, spinal muscular atrophy (SMA), a severe neuromuscular disorder, can be treated with gene replacement therapy targeting the SMN1 gene using adeno-associated viral vectors to deliver a functional copy of the gene.

Neurodegenerative Diseases: Gene therapy holds potential for treating neurodegenerative diseases such as Parkinson's disease, Alzheimer's disease, and amyotrophic lateral sclerosis (ALS). Strategies include enhancing neurotrophic factor expression, promoting neuronal survival, clearing protein aggregates, and modulating neuroinflammation to slow disease progression and preserve neuronal function.

Gene Editing Technologies: Emerging gene editing technologies, such as CRISPR-Cas9, offer precise and efficient tools for correcting disease-causing mutations or modulating gene expression in the CNS. Gene editing holds promise for treating genetic forms of epilepsy, Huntington's disease, and other neurological disorders by correcting or modifying pathogenic gene sequences.

Regulation of Gene Expression: Gene therapy can modulate gene expression levels using RNA interference (RNAi), antisense oligonucleotides (ASOs), or small interfering RNAs (siRNAs) to silence or regulate specific genes implicated in neurological disorders. This approach is being investigated for conditions like Huntington's disease, spinocerebellar ataxias, and familial amyloid polyneuropathy.

Optogenetics and Designer Receptors Exclusively Activated by Designer Drugs (DREADDs): Advanced gene therapy techniques leverage optogenetics and DREADDs to precisely control neuronal activity and neurotransmitter release in the brain. These tools enable researchers to manipulate neural circuits and study the underlying mechanisms of neurological disorders, paving the way for novel therapeutic interventions.

Challenges and Considerations: Despite its potential, gene therapy for neurological disorders faces challenges such as achieving efficient and safe gene delivery to target cells, minimizing off-target effects, addressing immune responses, and ensuring long-term therapeutic efficacy. Ethical considerations, regulatory approval, and accessibility also play crucial roles in the development and translation of gene therapy approaches for clinical use.

Many nervous system disorders are minimally responsive to existing treatments, but they are potential candidates for gene therapy, an approach that can correct the genetic abnormalities contributing to its pathogenesis at the molecular level. Gene therapy involves either the introduction of a replacement allele into cells to compensate for the loss of gene function or the silencing of the dominant mutant allele that is pathologic to cells.

Neurological disorders that impact the central nervous system (CNS), including Alzheimer's disease (AD), Parkinson's disease (PD), Huntington's disease (HD) and amyotrophic lateral sclerosis (ALS), and stroke are serious issues for both patients and clinicians because these disorders are typically difficult to treat with traditional pharmacological approaches once they develop due to late diagnosis, complexity of the nervous system and physical barriers that limit distribution of medications into CNS after peripheral administration. Patients with these disorders suffer from both symptoms and sequelae in their remaining lifetime. New strategies are progressively developed to overcome the unmet medical needs in conventional therapy.

Current Gene Therapy Approaches for Alzheimer's Disease

Strategy: Immunotherapy vaccine, Aβ degradation enzyme

Targeted genes: Aβ antibody, Aβ cDNA, Neprilysin

Therapeutic effects: Decreased Aβ deposition in AD mouse models, Decreased Aβ deposition, improved memory and cognition ability, Decreased Aβ deposition, oligomers, and alleviation of abnormal learning and memory in AD mouse model.

Current Gene Therapy Approaches for Parkinson's Disease

Strategy: Dopamine biosynthesis enzyme

Targeted genes: AADC

Therapeutic effects: Three phase I clinical trials for AAV2-AADC delivery into bilateral put amen reported alleviation of motor symptoms in moderate and advanced PD patients. Stable and persistent transgene expression for more than 4 years

Current Gene Therapy Approaches for Huntington's Disease

Strategy: Mutant HTT knockdown

Targeted genes: siRNA, shRNA, miRNA

Therapeutic effects: Reduced brain atrophy, neural inclusion, rescue of motor deficits, and increase in survival in HD mouse model. Complete elimination of mutant HTT-positive inclusions with improved behavioural deficits in HD mouse model. Nonallele-specific silencing of HTT showed improved motor coordination and survival in the HD mouse model.

Current Gene Therapy Approaches for Amyotrophic Lateral Sclerosis Disease

Strategy: Mutant SOD1 knock down, Nonsense-mediated mRNA decay, Reduction of build-up of C90RF72 repeat expansion RNA.

Targeted genes: shRNA, UPF1, ASO

Therapeutic effects: Delayed disease onset, expanded lifespan, enhanced survival of spinal motor neurons, and maintenance of neuromuscular junctions in ALS SOD1 rat model. Preservation of forelimb function and improved motor scores in ALS TDP-43 rat model. Reduced RNA foci generated by the expanded RNA in vitro.

Current Gene Therapy Approaches for Stroke Disease

Strategy: Anti-ischemia induced apoptosis. Neovascularization.

Targeted genes: NAIP, SAG, Bcl-2 and Bcl-n, IL-1

Therapeutic effects: Reduced ischemic damage in rat model. Reduced infarct areas where SAG was highly expressed. Delayed ischemia neuronal death, reduction in infarct size, and improvement in neurological function. Reduced cerebral infarct volume.

www.ingramcontent.com/pod-product-compliance
Lightning Source LLC
Chambersburg PA
CBHW071350230926
51846CB00002B/497
9789348734440